THE DIARY OF A BRIDE TO BE

BOOK 1

A REASON, A SEASON OR A LIFETIME

KATANDRA SHANEL JACKSON

FreedomInk
PO Box 1093 Reidsville, GA 30453

FreedomInk

Paperback ISBN 978-0-9896786-5-0

Printed in the United States of America

http://www.freedomink365.com

PREFACE

<u>S O   A M A Z I N G</u>

IT TRULY AMAZES ME TO SEE JUST HOW BEAUTIFUL LOVE IS

ONCE YOUR EYES ARE OPEN AND YOU SEE THAT YOU'VE BEEN

IN LUST ALL YOUR LIFE.

AND YOU THINK TO YOURSELF...

SO THIS IS WHAT LOVE LOOKS LIKE.

AMAZING!!!

ACKNOWLEDGEMENTS

Thanks in abundance my beautiful husband to be, Herman. For without you, the words that lay herein this book would have made for a different story. One whose ending shall remain uncertain. Fate and Destiny made sure of it, and I'm glad they did. Thanks for the insurmountable amount of love you have given me, in doing so you have healed a broken heart and mended a soul. Thank you for not only loving me, but for also loving the children we call 'ours'! I love you...

To my wonderful, beautiful, awesome children, Jermaine Trevon, Kailyn Elise and Ashley Vanique, thanks for being you; in doing so you have gradually transformed me. Each day is a challenge that I gladly rise to. You three make me a better person, a better woman, a better mother, a better bride to be. Thanks, Mommy loves each of you...

Exceptional Accolades at Sonya Lewis for keeping me company as I recalled these memories! I know you're always a call and a cup away, smile...

Family & Friends
This is a special note of thanks to those of you whom reside in our inner circle. Thanks for believing in something greater than each of us... Love!

Last but not least, Mom! How could I forget about you? Thanks for taking on both roles. Where would I be without you? Thanks for believing in me first!
I love you...

SPECIAL THANKS

Aunt Sheila T. Byrd & Aunt Petronyia McFadden   Sonya
& Shannia Lewis
Angel & Noah & Keylen Collins
Vernice & Roy Scott
Herman L. Taylor II
Shanara, Percy III, Percy IV,
Shanathan, & Phillip Brown

~

Thank each of you for making this book possible. Your contribution towards my vision is greatly appreciated. I'm especially grateful for Angel Wings

DEDICATION

I dedicate this book to the loves of my life...
Jermaine Trevon, Kailyn Elise & Ashley Vanique
&
The newest member of our little circle,
Herman
You all each in your own ways
have at some point, interchangeably
caressed my wounds,
captured my heart,
and captivated my soul.
Thanks for restoring
Love

Katandra Shanel...

A LETTER TO THE READER

Dear Reader,

How wonderful to share my story, your story, our story with the world! A little girl somewhere right now in this moment in time is dreaming of her happily ever after. And there is a little boy playing dungeons and dragons, he is the daring and dashing knight, just in time to save the damsel in distress! It's not always pink ponies and glass slippers, and the rescue may not always go as planned. The road can get a little bumpy and the ride discouraging at times, but know that as long as you believe, love will find a way! This story is for you......

The Diary Of A Bride To Be...

Katandra Shanel...

P.S Happy reading. Don't forget to follow up on the non fiction, romantic comedy. Check out The Diary of A Bride To Be Book 2: The Return of Spring. Available at Amazon, Barnes & Noble, Books-A-Million, where amazing books are sold! Contact the Author at katandra@freedomink365.com

14

INTRODUCTION

This book is about love...
The lessons learned therof,
the laughter that accompanies it
and the breath it breathes into a new life.
This is my journey.

Table of Contents

FALL

IT'S NOT 1915

May 3, 2010, Herman proposed to me, and I lovingly said yes! But we must not start there, for the beginning actually takes place sometime late summer / early fall 2009. We met online via Mocospace. Hey it's not 1915. July 2, 2009, we were on our way home from the National American Miss Georgia competition that was held downtown Atlanta. I was getting rather tired. The kids were asleep in the backseat and the radio was doing very little to keep me awake. I got online via my cellular... and yes I know you should not text and drive... and I don't! I found this website that seemed similar to MySpace, but perhaps more interesting. So I created a username, something simple that I would remember, kshanel. This site kept me occupied for the duration of the drive. It was not then that our cyber paths crossed. I actually cannot pinpoint the exact day and time. I just know that it changed my life forever.

A FRIEND REQUEST... ACCEPTED

Off and on Mocospace, usually when bored. I received a friend request from atl381. Ok. View. Seem interesting, intelligent, and handsome. Yet very far away... Atlanta!!! Wasn't that a 4 hour drive? But I thought, "What the hey, why not?" Friend request... accepted. Instant messages soon commenced. The occasional inbox message became less and less as phone numbers were exchanged. Due to my then mobile plan, I was not too keen on sending and receiving photo messages. But that never stopped an over eager friend from sending some very (ummmmmmm) revealing pics. The 1st conversation I can recall occurred on a Saturday night. His cousin was in Atlanta visiting and the two of them were out together with some friends. It was the first glimpse I had into a passion he holds dear... architecture. I remember sitting in the tub with my eyes closed imagining the surroundings he so vividly described. The marble fixtures, the fountains, the trees. With a very quiet entourage (his cousin and a few of his cousin's friend are hearing impaired), there was so much noise between he and I as we talked. That night he became more than a cyber-friend.

FRACTIONS, DECIMALS, AND POLYNOMIALS...
WHAT THE #*%^

Fall 2009, I was accepted into Georgia Southern University! My classes; Intro to Sociology (which to me was pleasantly similar to psychology- in a much broader sense of course), U.S government (which I loathed), FYE African Art, and Math... pre-algebra! Yeah you read right. Fractions, decimals, and polynomials... what the #*%^!!! Amidst a previous conversation, I recalled how math-y my new friend was, so I decided to tap his brain. Algebra, calculus, and trigonometry rolled off of his tongue like some foreign language, and unfortunately for me, I don't speak Portuguese! Still, he tried to explain to me in the simplest terms, that elusive beast that still eludes me.

OHH THE HORROR

Seconds, minutes, hours, and days passed, as did a few faces along the way. Still it never dissuaded the new found friendship between him and me. I was beginning to feel the weight of the world on my shoulders from being a single mother and a student and was in much need of a vacation! So he, knowing all I was juggling, extended an invitation for me to visit him in Atlanta. I was excited at the prospect. Immediately, I made arrangements for the children to spend a few days with an aunt and uncle. I packed my things and after classes ended on a Wednesday, I made a little (ummm, kinda long) trip. 16 West to 75 North, I made my way to Hapeville GA. There was an immediate physical attraction. He remembers that 1st kiss all too well... "Lemon kisses" he calls em. Actually, the flavor was tangerine! So commenced my 4 day weekend. He introduced me to his family (his niece and nephew were absolutely gorgeous). He took me on a tour of his city, 10 minutes from downtown Atlanta. We visited a local eatery, J. Buffalos, he frequented a lot then. All seemed to be going well, but it was here, that my perfect little daydream was shattered into a million pieces. Known by the locals, the waitress asked if I was his new girlfriend. You could literally see the horror on his face! Wow... Such a letdown I thought. Such a disappointment. It seemed the friendship was perfect and in each other's presence we got along great. Naturally, I assumed we would become more than friends. But boy was I wrong. Feeling somewhat crushed, I decided to exit stage right, while some dignity was still intact. I cut my visit short and spent the remainder of my vacation with a friend, mending a broken ego.

A FORK IN THE ROAD

After the upset of my little getaway, I returned home with a slightly bruised heart. The conversation between he and I became less frequent, and where a special friendship transpired, a fork in the road emerged. Mocospace logins became quite habitual out of sheer boredom. During these online visits I was becoming more and more acquainted with a particular user. I cannot recall his user i.d, and his name is quite unimportant now. We met & got along ok. And sad as the truth can be at times, the truth is, I was anxious for any opportunity to leave my hometown. I was invited to relocate to College Park, GA. During the weeks that followed, I thought a lot about Herman. I wondered how he was and what he might be up to, never failing to realize just how near he was, a mere 6 exits away...

FANCY MEETING YOU HERE!!!

Amidst a deteriorating relationship, I developed a zealous need for some space. So I began getting better acquainted with my surroundings, started making friends with the locals and just getting out in general. I took the train with a few friends one day, very unassuming and quite unsuspecting. I simply just needed to get out. So I'm sitting on the train in a seat nearest the door. The train's 1st stop was East Point, one station after College Park. The door opens, and lo and behold, a very startled Herman steps on. Then almost like a winter's snow melting at the mere hint of spring, any slights that had been administered, diminished in his presence. He sat beside me and we began talking as if months had never passed. He was curious to know how I came to be back in his city and I was curious to know what the resurface of his presence meant. Feeling for a slight moment, the pain of an open scar, I pushed the thought aside. So again, he and I once more became friends.

WINTER

ROOMATES BY ANY OTHER NAME

As winter's bite began to nibble, some things became quite evident to me! 1) Not all things were meant to last; 2) All things enter our lives for a reason, a season, or a lifetime; and 3) Sometimes it's better to be friends then to become enemies. Mid January I found myself faced with a tough decision, one that would require some divine intervention or the defeat of a dreamer. The latter did not prevail. I moved in with Herman during the 1st days of February due to none other but divine intervention. I mean to go from finding to falling in then falling out to finding again... Confusing I know. This would be my state for the weeks to follow. Still, Herman had become a great friend, rushing deliberately to my rescue when I needed a friend more than anything. I knew the silent wants that would accompany this new level of our friendship and everyone naturally assumed that me moving in meant that we were dating. No one really believed that we were only roommates... But we were, weren't we?

COMING ON WAYYYYY TOO STRONG!

As the title has it, yes, you guessed it. This is exactly what I did! And sad as it seems, all advances were ill met by an unwilling, kicking & screaming Herman... Ok, ok... So I'm exaggerating, just a little. Needless to say, his feelings about me had not changed over the course of a season. Still, this did not dissuade me in the least. I truly felt that he would come around. So I batted my lashes sweetly, laughed very demurely. You get the point. I threw in every flag I could, each one shouting "I like you!" Nothing! Then to make matters worse, he became the occasional, habitual flirt.

Recap: girl meets boy, girl likes boy, boy insane, turns girl down, girl moves in, still likes boy, boy still crazy, sometimes flirts, girl confused...

CHEESECAKE... ON THE HOUSE

I suppose it goes without saying that roommates became rather close. It was as if we had been the best of friends forever. My advances continued but not as they were before. It was almost like I knew then what he kept denying. And deny he did. Still this never stopped us from hanging out. I dunno if you could call it a 'date' back then though. We agreed to be each other's valentine, him having had unfavorable valentines in previous years and myself not remembering ever having a valentine. We made reservations and because he had to work Valentine's Day, we had a pre-valentine dinner that Thursday. The location? Buckhead... The atmosphere? Ritzy... The restaurant? Chops... My immediate response? Niiiiccceeeeee!!! Dinner came complete with valet parking, heated entry and our very own Mr. Belvedere type waiter; you know the one that pulls your seat out, pushes you in closer to the table, and lays the napkin across your lap, yeah, one of those types. I gifted my then roomie with a blue and black bag, very masculine. Inside was a set of multi-colored, glass photo coasters (each with a photo of me inserted), a pair of Family Guy boxers (with the football headed baby... He loves that crazy show), and his favorite candy, snickers. And his gift to me that evening, the night, I felt as if I owned it! We had so much fun. I watched in complete terror and amazement as he devoured a steak the size of a platter. I fell in love with crab cakes that night... they were delicious. For dessert, our more than gracious waiter served us cheesecake, on the house. It was a sweet ending to a brilliant night. All was perfect until... As we prepared to leave, the table Herman jostled with his knees the entire night tipped as he stood, and let's just say the ride home was cold and wet... Very... Cold and wet!

LOVE IS AS LOVE DOES

The weeks that followed held a few special surprises for me. The 1st came in the form of my weakness. Earrings! A pair of sterling silver hoops with interchangeable charms; blue K's, green clovers, a puppy, and a camera. Seems Mr. Taylor and a close friend of his went to Buckhead with me in mind. He personally selected the earrings and charms, and I loved them, I still do. They happen to be my favorite pair! A few weeks later, I received a phone call on my way home. My "roomie" was acting extra weird. Seems he wanted me to stop by his sister's place. So I did. She and I talked a bit, but I must admit, she was acting way weird too, almost like they didn't want me to go home. As anxious as I was getting, I waited patiently. Then, a phone call, "You can come home now." Ummm, ok. So I commenced to make my way home, unlocked the door, and there he is all dapper and debonair in his suit and tie with flowers in hand. The setting was picturesque. He had just finished preparing dinner, a sentimental effort; he's still learning his way around the kitchen. There is a bottle of chilled sparkling grape juice, the table is romantically set for two, and the music is low. In the bedroom there are a million chocolate candy Kisses on the bed in the shape of a heart and butterfly! He tells me to relax. A bath had been run, and the candlelight gave the roses amongst the bubbles a real ambiance. I was shocked but not surprised. He was in that moment the man I fell in love with! I spent the rest of the evening in his presence, enjoying his determinations, and wondering if he had finally fallen in love with me as well.

THIS CALLS FOR A DIVERSION!

It is what it is. The more I professed my feelings, the more complicated things became between friends. So I decided it was time to let that phantom go and seek something more concrete. Mocospace? Yep, you guessed it. The social website began to occupy idle time. To my temporary delight, I made a few "friends", none worth mentioning. A few had potential, but none captivated my senses the way.... Still, I was determined to make the most outta each distraction. Turns out, each was a disappointment. I began to redirect my attention on myself and my dreams. Started hanging out alone; parks, museums, book stores and the local library became my solace. And I was grateful for the diversion!

SPRING

HOME SWEET HOME OR HUMBLE BEGINNINGS?

A birthday celebration called for a mini vacation! So my roommate and I packed our things and headed for southeast Georgia to visit my hometown, a very small, very rural Manassas; A place of humble beginnings. The very place I loathed as a kid and made plans to escape one day. Now here I was returning. Home sweet home! I figured Herman too, would immediately loathe this place, but to my disdain he took pleasure in my plight. Go figure! The getaway consisted of a string of introductions to my familial ties, an up close and personal weekend with my children, an in your face encounter with a few crazy dogs, a couple of horses, some cows, and an insane goat. We made a trip to Tybee Island, enjoyed dinner out with Herman's cousin and the kids and paid a visit to the creek. I had begun entertaining thoughts outside of my obsession, so naturally I was somewhat caught off guard by the melting ice.

AND AS THE RETURN OF SPRING THREATENED
WINTER, THE ICE BEGAN TO MELT

And melt it did. It was as if someone shed light into a very dark room and all was becoming clear. But it was all too much for me, as I was greatly displeased by the unexpected twist. The 1st sign of spring occurred March 27th. Herman celebrated his 29th birthday with me surrounded by my family in my hometown, a very special and unselfish gesture; it was in his eyes. His birthday gift, a 'Claxton' t-shirt and a photo album I had taken great care in selecting and starting with a few photos. He loved it, of course. As I reveled in a moment of thanks, with the clamor of my beautiful children in the background, he looked at me with such intensity. It was in his eyes! So many things it seemed he wanted to finally scream. Instead his eyes whispered, and I being the intuitive woman that I am heard the words of his heart loud and clear, still... It was so unexpected. I actually chided myself for being so optimistic. After all, this was my roomie and I had finally come to terms that it would never be more than that. After I dismissed the 'look' there was a moment! You know the kinda moment that entangles feelings and emotions, a moment that's so undeniable no matter how hard you try to shake it, you can't. It happened at the creek. It had been raining like crazy so the bank was completely covered and a cold front accompanied the rain. As we stood side by side, I spoke of times my children and I had spent there. An awkward silence, then firm but gentle hands pulled me nearer into the sweetest embrace & roommates kissed as lovers do. And as the chill in the air disappeared, I knew spring had returned!

I HEREBY DUB YOU, GODFATHER...

Spring break week, the kids came to visit. We had so much fun. They had a chance to do some sightseeing, and they like me, fell in love with the city of Atlanta! Herman was a more than gracious host, allowing his inner child to interact with my children. We took them to our favorite restaurant, La Fiesta! The kids had fruit smoothies in pretty, party glasses. Herman and I had our faves; his, tequila sunrise and mine, amaretto sour. The evening was perfect. Earlier that day I mentioned I had a very important announcement to make. During dinner I dubbed Herman, Godfather. To my delight all were pleased. I could not have found a better person to bestow this honor unto. My roommate had become my bestfriend, my children were enchanted by him, and I was glad!

AND THE TABLES TURNED, SURPRISE SURPRISE... NOT

Prior to the look and the moment, I was absolutely gaga over my then roomie. I kept telling him, "The moment I move on, you're gonna come around." He thought I was mildly if not very insane. He simply laughed each time I made this statement. His trip back home with me was great, and the kids coming up for spring break was awesome as well. The Saturday before the kids left, we decided to have a barbeque at Sweetwater Creek. Don't ask where it's at. All I know is that it's somewhere off of 1-20... I think, see what I'm saying. The setting was spectacular. The creek which was more like a lake was beautiful. The kids, mine and his sisters, played together. My eldest, helped his sister get things started on the grill as I nervously attempted to distract myself. Herman and a very close friend of his had just gotten off of work and were en route. This put me meeting his family without him which was somewhat awkward. I did my best to dismiss this uncomfortable feeling by telling myself "We're just roommates... We're just roommates... We're just roommates." I'm still not sure if anyone ever believed this, including myself. His family seemed cool, one family is just like the next and this one fit the bill. Still, I was overjoyed when the car rounded the bend. Herman had arrived. The food was almost done, they were just in time. I, being on slight edge noticed something at that gathering that pretty much freaked me out. My roomie was extra touchy-feely. The closeness never bothered me before. It's probably one of the things that aided my confusion. But in front of the kids, his sister, and those that I had just met, I mean it really freaked me out. Just as I had come to a comfortable resting place at this crossroad and was finally ok with this 'friendship'... Here he was making it something more. And the tables turned. I would like to report that this change surprised me, but it did not. What it did though was infuriate me!

"RING, RING, RING... HELLO?"

AN UNEXPECTED CALL PART 1

The following weeks consisted of him in my shoes and me in his. His advances were ill met, as I was attempting to maintain the 'friendship'. What a twist! This conflict made for a strained environment. We never argued before, but we began to have these, I dunno, lovers spats... Whatever they were, I spent a lot of time sitting on the bathroom floor with him on the opposite side of the door. And he spent a lot of time across the tracks at an abandoned gas station. This tug-of-war was really beginning to get the best of us. Herman spent the evening with an associate; I think it was a Thursday and I must admit his absence was an unpleasant event. To think, the man I absolutely adored was out with another woman. This was not ok with me. It got my wheels turning if not my blood boiling. A few days later I decided I needed some alone time. It was the Saturday that I will never forget. I got directions, hopped on the train, and headed to Buckhead's Lennox Mall. It had begun to rain when I made it to my destination, but this was ok. I intended to take my time. It was just what I needed to clear my head... Think... Reflect... Drive myself insane. Walking around Belks, my phone began to ring! "Ring, ring, ring... Hello? Hi dad!" it was my father. A brief history on he and I: We don't have a very strong bond. We're more like strangers in passing than father & daughter. I have come to accept this. Odd as it is, the almost non-existent relationship we do or don't have makes it easy to talk to him. He is never judgmental, always giving his unbiased 'from experience' opinion. So the call was quite welcome. Besides I was so lost in my own head, I needed someone to pull me back. Nice rescue. So back to the call. He was just calling to inquire as to how I had been. Having spoken to him several weeks before, he was pretty caught up on my current state of mind. So I further filled him in. Letting him know of this predicament I was in. And unsurprisingly to my surprise, I found the answer I had been seeking, hidden amongst a string of questions! "What kind of guy is he..? How does he treat you...? Does he respect you as a woman..? How does he feel about the kids...? Does he want more...? Can you imagine the rest of your life with him...? Can you imagine the rest of your life without him...? Do you love him...? Are you in love with him...? Is he your friend first & foremost and last but not least.......?" Then it dawned on me, I was crazy in love with my bestfriend! "Ring, ring, ring... Hello? Hi Herman..."

"RING, RING, RING... HELLO?"

AN UNEXPECTED CALL PART 2

My heart fluttered as he answered the phone, odd, that had never happened before! As nervous as I was, I was determined to let him know that yes, we were reading from the same book... And at long last we had arrived at the same page! Needless to say, he was surprised but happy at my change of mind, whereas my heart had never faltered. It was a very scary moment for me! It was a moment of surrendering to something greater than myself, love. This was what I had been longing for! To hear those coveted three words, "I love you". He loves me? Wow! Never before had I felt that way. All around me it stormed as I put my trust in him and let love. The weather had gotten worse but inside I was at peace! My nerves eased as we talked and within mere minutes it felt as if we had been together forever. That still gets me sometimes. So different yet so alike, I wasn't quite sure how we were gonna make it work, but determined we were!

OPPOSITES ATTRACT? OBVIOUSLY!!!

As I previously stated, Herman and I had our similarities but for sure we were nothing alike! Coming from an astrological standpoint we're not exactly compatible. Him being a ram headed Aries and me being a sexy, secretive, seductive Scorpio! I tried to ignore this despite the fact that yes, I'm very into my signs. Also, Herman is pretty outgoing as where I am more the loner type. He will dance at the drop of a good base line. As for me, I prefer to cut a rug alone, all alone, I'm kinda shy like that. His spending style is $$$$ and mine is $, hey what can I say? This girl loves a good sale... "Clearance rack here I come!". These are just to name a few. It's kinda hard to explain each difference, I just knew that they were there, and suddenly this awareness made me a bit doubtful. Then again I had to remember all the ways we were alike... Loving so many of the same things! Music, good food, movies. Perhaps all it really takes is one commonality. We think alike. Scary? I know! I never gave much thought as to how much opposites attract... But they do... Obviously!

HOW COULD MY PLEASURE CAUSE SO MUCH PAIN

Everything that followed happened rather fast after that stormy day. One minute we were on the phone deciding we should be together, the next he was proposing, but let me not get ahead of myself! It seemed just as my pleasure was setting in, others were not as pleased. This caused me great pain. Not because I care what others think of me and the choices I make, but more so because I have always been a happy-go-lucky kinda gal, never letting too much get to me. But I must admit this was! I assumed all would be happy for us, but I was wrong. Guess I was so caught up in the moment that I forgot to take the feelings of others into consideration! He assured me over and over again that all would be fine, that his love for me was strong & steadfast. Phew! What a relief. As I think back I'm a bit embarrassed at how my behavior must have come across to him. Here I was one minute this tough chic with mild attitude, black nail polish, and 10 + tattoos, completely falling apart on him like some frail, wounded, sick thing! Wow! "Who is this person?" I wondered. Definitely not the woman he would soon propose to...

HEARTS HAVE SPOKEN

I may not be the choice some understand or the choice others would have opted. But his heart chose me just the same. Not on some fly by the minute whim or some hasty & careless decision. Hearts thought hard and long, and in the end... love won.

A NOT SO FAIRYTALE PROPOSAL...

2 dozen red roses, horse drawn carriage, him in suit in tie... record scratch! The way he proposed didn't exactly come out of some fairytale! What it did come from though was his heart! It was the 1st Monday in May, May 3rd to be exact, and Herman and I were lounging around, me in my pajamas and him in t-shirt and a pair of blue, plaid boxers. My mind was St. Elsewhere. A proposal was the furthest thing from it. Then suddenly, a 6'4 shadow cast over me and before I could look up he had gotten down on one knee... And my heart skipped a beat, or two. Hey who am I kidding? It completely stopped! For once in my entire life, the writer was speechless. He took me by the hand and proposed ever so chivalrously. It was not exactly a Cinderella moment... It was however, his way. Forever surprising me! Even today it makes me laugh, the thought I had after the initial shock."Ya gon' propose to me in ya boxers? Really? Wow! Ya gotta be kiddin me! Is this the story that we are to tell our grandchildren one day?" And that's how it happened. That's the story of my not so fairytale proposal!

A BIRTHDAY CELEBRATION!!!

May 6th, Herman and I packed a suitcase and headed down south to celebrate my youngest daughter's 7th birthday. I was extra, extra, did I say extra??? Excited! This would be the 1st major event he and I would attend as a couple! We were not hanging out with the family as roommates, but as something much, much more! I was curious as to the reactions I was sure to receive. Mind you, I was not anxious in the least; after all, my Herman is such the gentleman! Safely there, we picked up the kids, made a few rounds, and headed to Statesboro that evening. The following day, a Friday, yeah it's another one of those that I will never forget, we attended my eldest, 7th grade end of year field day. It was awesome! Herman was introduced to my bestest gal pal. We had a blast as we watched the rigorous play of adolescents. Afterward we made our way back to Statesboro. I wanted to stop by Frills and Fancy, a formal attire boutique. Dare I say it? Wedding dresses! Up to the 3rd floor my heart was racing with excitement. I chose a number of dresses to try on, steering clear of the poufy dresses. Herman also chose a number of dresses for me to try on. Sadly, his selections way outdid mine; one in particular, a pretty, poufy, ballroom, Cinderella type dress. I frowned at the initial selection, and then fell in love all over again upon looking into his eyes as he watched me emerge from the dressing parlor. A plethora of emotions were there. Was this the dress? Perhaps! The next day we revisited Tybee Island, this time the weather was perfect! Sunday before we left for Atlanta we gathered at Altamaha Park for a birthday celebration. We had so much fun as family and friends alike showed up for the birthday festivity. That evening after saying our goodbyes, Herman and I made our way back to I-16. As usual I was gonna miss my babies, but I couldn't wait to get back to Atlanta!

IT FIT LIKE A GLOVE... HMMMMMM!!!

Back to the city with a few weeks left of what I deemed, a pre wedding honeymoon! The kids were still in my hometown and had a few short weeks left in school before summer let in. Herman and I were determined to make the most out of these fleeting days. We knew how fast they would pass and life as we had gotten accustomed was about to change, of course for the best, smile! Those days comprised of walks at the park, hanging out with friends, staying out late, a few movies, a couple of dinner dates, and just being with each other. I rather relished these days. The most memorable to me is hanging out in Buckhead one evening. The entire day was perfect. I awoke bright and early to a kiss; Herman was on his way to work. Once the door closed behind him, I lay across the bed in wonderment. "What to eat? What to eat?" I wasn't really feeling cereal or oatmeal, and was not up for cooking either. I guess one thought led to another and that thought became a dream as I drifted back to sleep! In between sleep and consciousness, I heard the door open. I sleepily opened my eyes, and there's Herman with breakfast! McDonald's... Breakfast burritos and orange juice. How sweet! My day commenced as Herman and I did lunch together that afternoon, a rare occasion! I excitedly awaited his arrival home that evening as we had plans to go to hang out. So we're in Buckhead and I have been going on and on for weeks, "What's all the buzz about Starbucks?", so of course this is our 1st stop and now I know... I absolutely loved it. It is a coffee lover's haven. We played around in the World Market, then made our way to Demetrias! Ok, for those of you not in the know, Demetrias has some of the most perfectest wedding dresses! I had only seen ads in bridal magazines and I half assumed it was in some big shot place like the Big

51

Apple (New York). But here it was in the Big Peach (Georgia). We went in, looked around and I fell in love! That's exactly how it happened. An attendant pulled the dress from the rack; we headed to the dressing parlor, bustier on, stepped into the dress and to my surprise no clips were needed to secure the back! It zipped! This dress was obviously made for me! It fit like a glove... Hmmmmmmmm! Herman however was not as enamored as I was with the dress. Little secret, the attendant suggested I leave his butt home next time. Besides isn't it bad luck to see the bride in her wedding dress before the big day? Whole Foods Market was the last stop, or so I thought. This store was stocked with everything. A hundred different kinda nuts, fish the length of my arm, and fruit. The store was perfectly stocked. I found everything except New England clam chowder! Wow. Really? Back on our side of town, I found what i was looking for. Over clam chowder and a movie, we ended the night on a most perfect note!

SUMMER

SINK OR SWIM

I knew that our cute and cozy couple hood was about to come abruptly to an end. School was out and summer had let in. The children were ready to make their transition. We made our way back to southeast Georgia yet again, this time the ride back promised to be a bit livelier! The kids had done really well in their studies, and each was rewarded with a promotion! This was perfect timing for a change in their lives... But the life I was most concerned with was not theirs or my own, but that of Herman's! I knew the kids would be ok with the move once they got used to the city and started making new friends. But he was the one being thrown into the deep end of parentsville! "Please let him swim and not sink." Prior encounters proved that he was great with the kids, but this was a beast of a different nature, interaction with each other would not be brief. I knew just how detrimental it could be, if for some reason Herman began to drown. Much to my delight he took to this new territory like a fish to water. Looked like clear skies and easy sailing for all. The U.S.S Jackson-Taylor would stay afloat!

NO TIME TO POST

I suppose it goes without saying that the kids relocating to Atlanta pretty much tied up all the free time that I had once cherished. With a full calendar scheduled out, I planned to make the most of summer. Herman was impressed that I had decided to do some mini lessons with the kids while school was not in session! The idea of them not doing something constructive made me cringe! The kids and I hung out at the park and library. We even made it to the High Museum! A few weeks later, my son had a sickle cell crisis and had to spend a few days in the hospital. This didn't dampen his or our spirits. The best part of early summer to me was hanging out at the movies with the kids! The original plans were to catch Karate Kid at Buckhead's Fork and Screen. Lo and behold, they were sold out. So instead of dinner and a movie, we had dinner, then a movie! This worked out great. Except my fiancé had a chance to see 1st hand the melt down of a Drama Queen! What? Not me. My eldest daughter and second born! Aside from that, the movie was great and the evening ended with three beautiful, sleeping children in the backseat and the love of my life beside me!

TWO WHOLE WEEKS

Wow! Two weeks? Two whole weeks! Sweet. The kids decided they wanted to spend 2 weeks of their summer vacation back home. So we packed their bags, loaded up the truck, and at 6:45 a.m., we headed southeast. Their uncle met us in Dublin. We made the exchange and parted, traveling in opposite directions. I looked into my rearview and wished for the safe continuation of my crew's journey; and as they pulled farther outta sight, I breathed a soft, sweet sigh. I would miss them but two weeks would be over all too soon. Two weeks? Two whole weeks! Wow!

PAINTING THE NAILS OF A PORCELAIN DOLL

Back and forth spending more time with his sister and her family! Hey. What can I say? I was missing the kids just a little! Herman's niece has a doll with dare I say it, no feet! How sad. What was even sadder were the clothes that hung from her body. They looked like the threadbare clothes that would have been on the back of a runaway slave, I kid you not! Wait is that funny? Ok it is, just a little! Come to find out, the doll came to its owner in its existing special condition, missing a leg. But you know mommies and their babies... We love em at first sight no matter what! Seeing the love for this ragged doll in the eyes of a little girl, made me want to doctor on her. You know, stethoscope, check... scalpel, check... Legs? Any who, I asked permission to take this doll into my care, I had plans for her! Her owner was kind enough to trust me with her 'baby'. Thanks! So Herman and I took 'Rudy' home, and I immediately went to work. I gathered all the tools it seemed necessary to doctor on this special doll! Thread, needle, cotton, and some new clothes for crying out loud! Herman played a video game, while I worked diligently, and diligently I did work. I wrapped quilt batting around the wire where her leg had once been and bent the end ever so lightly. Tada... Feet! I slid a pair of green and white striped baby socks around the cotton and sewed those bad boys on tight... Just in case a little girl's curiosity got the better of her! Next I cut a pair of mint green, infant pants that transformed themselves into a dress. Believe me, I had little to do with this! It was like hand, needle, and thread were one! I was oblivious to the dolls fragile state aside from her previous condition. I touched her face when I was done, only to find out she was porcelain! What a delightful surprise. I wet a rag, soaped it lightly, and washed Rudy's face. Last but not least, I painted the tiny fingernails of a porcelain doll, pink.

OREO MUDSLIDE WASTED!

Not a moment of free time was wasted. Herman and I went out the same night we dropped the kids off. Moms need a break too. 'Twilight Eclipse' at Fork and Screen, unfortunately the show was sold out! So we went to see 'Grown Ups' instead. It was great, as if I expected it to be lame! Adam Sandler, Chris Rock, and a few more of Hollywood's funniest men. The movie was a riot! I loved the theatre as well. We found perfect seats and ordered before the movie began! There were a few interesting items on the menu... And I wanted to try something different, so I ordered a shrimp pizzetta and a pomegranate martini. Delicious! He had quesadillas, big surprise! The best part of the evening aside from being with my honey was dessert. Yummy! Oreo mudslide (she licks lips) laced with vodka. Who wants to get oreo mudslide wasted?

A BRIEF INTERLUDE:

10 things I love about him
1. His smile. It's so genuine.
2. His intelligence. I love that big beautiful brain of his.
3. His persistence when determined.
4. His sincerity.
5. His humor.
6. His height. Yes his height!
7. His spirit.
8. His appetite for life.
9. His view of the world.
10. His kisses...

The list is infinite. These are just a few things I love about him, not to be mistaken with why, for love is truly immeasurable!

<u>MY BESTFRIEND</u>

HE IS MY HEART'S BEAT
MY MINDS EVERY WAKING THOUGHT
MY SUBCONCIOUS DREAMS SOUGHT
HE IS THE BREATH I BREATHE
MY SIGHT, SMELL, TASTE, TOUCH
MY "LOVE YOU SO MUCH!"
HE IS MY SUN, MOON, AND STARS
THE YANG TO MY YEN
HE IS
MY BESTFRIEND

KATANDRA SHANEL...

I AM...

Listening to:
Shadow of Day- Linkin Park. I'm in a rock star mood.

Reading:
Dirty Money by Mel Cebulash aloud to my honey.

Excited about:
A night alone with Herman, that and Tex Mex salad!!!

Wondering:
When the next poem will strike...

Craving: His love!!!

Wearing:
Gray pants, a new gray striped tee, white flip flops, and
my favoritist earrings (the silver hoops).

Dreaming:
About the day I become Mrs.

STONECREST at LITHONIA

Herman and I took his sister to lunch at one of our favorite spots, The Vortex located at Little Five Points, Atlanta! See look at me learning my way around. As usual there was a change of plans as we were to do lunch at the Melting Pot.....ummmmmm! But someone decided not to call ahead and when we got there at 1:30 p.m. they hadn't opened yet! So back to the Vortex, it promised to be interesting the 2nd time around for myself. The 1st time I was in an ill mood, but this day was on a much happier note until... A phone call! No details are needed here, lets just say I was tempted to forgo lunch and make my way south, not well rested I might add. Pure aggravation! Thankfully Herman was there. Funny how we balance each other out! Whereas I can be raging mad, he calms me, and he can be in an unpleasant mood, and I mellow him out. Anywho. Despite the phone call and my attention in another place, we made the most of lunch, and I still got a little teaser, melted cheese and fries. Hey I know it wasn't the Melting Pot, but it deliciously sufficed! After taking his sister back home, I was quietly informed that we were not done for the evening. The day was still young and he really wanted to take me someplace else! Where? I had no idea, and I absolutely hate surprises. I mean I loathe them. But he wasn't telling. We gassed up and were on our way. I sat anxiously on the passenger side, in an anxious fit of pain! We rode what seemed like forever, the city disappeared behind us, the scenery got very suburb-like. Finally we approached what looked like familiar territory, a mall! What delight! We walked and talked, the environment was very still even though we weren't far from the city! I really liked it. We got pretzels and frozen drinks. His, fruity and mine caffeinated! I guess one mall is just like another unless, there is an

'Icing by Claire's' in it!!! Ah ah ah ahhhhh (the sounds of the heavens parting). We walked in and I was in earring utopia! So many colors, styles, and choices... I was like a kid in a candy store. Happily lost! My honey helped me pick out 2 pair of earrings; one pair with blue, green, and purple feathers that hung from my ears, down my neck on mini chains. The other pair, cream enamel butterflies adorned with earth tone baubles!!! How pretty, both pair. Much to my liking, there was a cinema attached to the mall... And I got a chance to see Twilight Eclipse, finally! Stonecrest at Lithonia was fun!

2 WEEKS NOTICE INTERRUPTED

The call I received at The Vortex led Herman and I to southeast GA to pick up the crew a week early! Seems they were missing Atlanta and bored outta their minds! Talk about the winds of change. One minute they couldn't bear the thought of leaving the country, the next they couldn't wait to get back to the city. Kids! Go figure. Herman and I were glad to oblige their request to interrupt our 2 weeks on such short notice.

MANY ANGELS PART 1

1/2 volunteering and 1/2 volunteered, I met my mother a few miles past Macon to pick up my grandfather. My son decided to stay at home while the girls accompanied me, my mother was glad to see them. The return trip consisted of my grandparents, an uncle, a cousin, my girls, and a partridge in a pear tree. While my Papa kept his eyes peeled for a specialty shop and the girls played in the backseat alongside my grandmother, I listened closely to the sound of the interstate being assaulted by 4 tires. At least that's all I was hoping to hear. After making a quick stop, I thought to myself, "This highway is awfully loud, but just in case..." I pulled over onto the median, walked around the truck, checking all tires! All seemed fine to the naked eye, little did I know mayhem was toiling laboriously in a big pot. Driving further along, the sound of the interstate got louder and then, "Powwww!" The tire? Grip the steering wheel, calm everyone down, avoid the flow of traffic, ease onto the median, and get outta the truck. Tire indeed! My immediate thought, I was glad all were ok. My next immediate thought, my honey was at work without a way to me! Now what? After letting him know my predicament and locale, I frantically searched my contacts to see if anyone could lend a hand. No one! Just as despair was beginning to set in, a gold car pulled in front of where we were. A lady stepped out and asked if we needed any help! I text her license plate to Herman before getting into her car. Side note kids, never take rides offered by strangers. I was moving on faith that all would be fine, and if not, I was sure I could take the lady!

Arriving safely at my destination, I thanked the lady for the ride, but not before she asked for money for doing a deed from the goodness of her heart! Herman was already there. A good friend of his had taken an early lunch break to aid in my rescue. We checked a few local tire shops. The first returned no results, aside from a junkyard dog! No, really! A calm but vicious looking pit, female, all white. She was pretty. Pretty dangerous I'm sure! I was lost in a sea of thoughts as I walked toward a broken down Durango, same model as mine, eyeing the rims when all the guys started yelling, "Stop... Stop... Stop!" it took me a moment to realize they were screaming at me. Can you imagine my horror when I saw the reason why they were so hysterical? Back to the rescue in progress. At the next tire shop we found what we were looking for. Herman's friend had to be back to work by that time, so he let us keep his truck until said emergency was finite! Herman and I returned to exit 230 to pick up a very irritable entourage. As we approached the truck, emergency roadside assistance was arriving at the scene as well. Wow, what an on time blessing! He assisted us in removing a resistant dodge rim. With family and a blown tire in tow, we headed downtown Atlanta to the bus station. After dropping off the Detroit crew, we doubled back to the tire shop, had a new tire put on the rim, and the rest is history!

LOOKING

With our living arrangements becoming more and more claustrophobic, we were on the hunt for a larger abode in which to dwell. A few homes very near the airport caught our eye, but to me these homes seemed very expensive! Not to mention, I didn't feel we were quite prepared for that phase. So we turned our attention to rental homes and apartments in the area. We didn't wanna get too far away from Herman's job, so we contained the search within a specific radius. While surfing the internet one day, we discovered an ad for a nearby apartment that was leasing 3 bedrooms. The location was perfect, not far from his job. A phone call to the rental agent led to a visit to view said apartments. They really were perfect. It was within walking distance of both elementary and middle schools. Grocery stores conveniently neighbored the apartments, which were safely gated off from the remainder of the community and had 24 hour security, all at a reasonable price. Perfect, just perfect. We were done looking!

ABANDONED

He dropped me off in Manassas, closed the door, pressed the gas, and sped away! Maybe I'm exaggerating a little, ok, maybe a lot. Still, no matter how many times I replay it, my recollection of being away from him for the 1st time since saying "Yes" was excruciating. He drove 1/2 way, put me out to walk the other 1/2, closed the door, pressed the gas, and sped away! Ok, I admit, it happened nothing like that, but in my mind, the event was traumatic just the same. 75 South bound, again, with the children in tow. The route the same, but the purpose behind it not. Scheduled to move into our apartment the following Saturday, we planned to wrap up a few loose ends in South East GA. The children and I were to stay with my parents for a week. While there, I'd be paying a few bills and most importantly, closing out a storage unit. The ride was awful! The kids were not any more rambunctious than usual and Herman was his charming self, but I was a wreck. Nervous. Terrified at best! I didn't know what to expect while absent one another. Old hurts resurfaced, "Outta sight... Outta mind", echoed more fervently the closer we got to our destination. Sensing my uneasiness, Herman decided to stay a night. I don't know if this made matters better or worst! That evening passed all too quickly, still I relished every moment! The warmth of his skin next to mine, the scent of him in my nostrils, the sound of his heartbeat, his voice, his breath, his laughter. In a trance, I was lulled to sleep. The next morning he got into the truck, closed the door, pressed the gas, and abandoned me.

THE LONGEST NIGHT

It began as soon as he drove away. The quickened pulse, the racing heart, the sweat beads, the sudden chill! Wait! This is not supposed to be a horror story. Ok, the separation put me on edge, but I tried to dismiss this feeling by thinking "Hey, what are a few days?" Unlucky for me, it seemed as if time was suspended in space. Seconds felt like hours. How was I to survive days? Herman left behind upon my request, the shirt he had worn the day before. I wish I could report that I slept peacefully that 1st night without him, but I did not. Instead I lay there in the dark listening to the strange sounds of my rural environment all around me. Anyone who has ever lived in the country knows the noises I speak of. No matter how many sheep I attempted to count, sleep just would not come! When I finally began to feel that which had eluded me on what was the longest night, traces of a new day threatened to creep into the dark room. I tucked my chin into the collar of his shirt, closed my eyes, and as I inhaled I missed him even more!

1 WEEK...2 WEEKS... 1 WEEK I'M CONFUSED!

As I previously stated, the duration of my stay back home was only supposed to last 1 week. Then I spoke with Herman and got a little bad news! Seems although the paperwork was complete and processed, the apartment was not quite ready and would not be by that Friday! The earliest time it would be available to move into was that following Wednesday! My heart sank. I was so looking forward to the return of my honey, that the days actually began to move in real time. Saddened, nonetheless, I busied myself. I continued cleaning the storage unit, boxing and reboxing toys, clothes and books, donating to Goodwill that which no longer served a purpose for us, and just plain ol' throwing some things away. This was a new life, in a new place! I had no intentions of unnecessarily cluttering it. Upon checking my email one evening I was delighted to discover that my 1 week that unexpectedly turned into 2 weeks had become 1 week again. I was confused! Happy, but confused.

HE WAS TAKING CARE OF BUSINESS

Herman was busy at work managing the details of our move. I learned that along with a new place was a new school district. No longer did I have weeks to prepare the kids for the end of summer. School was to start in this new district within a few short days. Herman miraculously made it so, that we could move in exactly on the scheduled move in date! I heard the truck before I saw it. I think I sensed his presence near! I ran outside barefoot, to greet him. The kids were not far behind. We were all excited about the move. All within a matter of hours, he drove from Atlanta and picked us up. We cleared the storage out, said our goodbyes, and were on our way back. It was a long trip, doing 55 mph on the interstate, courtesy of U-Haul, with a trailer in tow. Then there was a detour 15 miles outside of our destination. Everyone was exhausted when we finally made it to his sister's house. The kids fell asleep immediately. As for Herman and I the excitement of our 1st apartment together was too great to sleep!

JUMPING UP AND DOWN

Friday finally, move in day, the morning came fast after we fell asleep. Up way too early. The apartment office opened at 9 a.m., and we were up at 7, out by 7:30... now what? Even though we could barely contain the excitement of the day, we managed to (im) patiently wait. We spent the first half of the morning at the park. I walked the trail, Herman played on the swings with the kids. Then we grabbed a bite to eat, breakfast, a rare treat seeing as how we are not exactly morning people and we usually catch lunch hours! We arrived at the apartments at 8:59, ok, maybe it was 9:01. I'm not sure who was more excited, me, Herman, or the kids. We put our signatures on the leasing agreement and got the keys to our 1st apartment together! The residence we previously inhabited was a one room studio. One bed, one sofa sleeper, a one sided sink, a mini stove top with 2 burners, one corner table and 2 chairs, a fridge and microwave, a television of course, and a bathroom. Sound like a lot? Well, before Herman inherited a fiancé and three children, it was plenty of room, for 1! Still, the summer months in that room built for 1 were torture! It felt like a 10x10 cage by the time 5 exited stage at right. Enter our new apartment. 3 bedrooms, 2 full baths, walk in closets, a laundry room, outside storage, private balcony, a spacious kitchen and living room and enough space for 5! We turned on all the lights, checked the water, flushed toilets, laid on the newly placed carpet, and inhaled that of fresh paint, breathing in the sweet scent of 'home'! After reality set in, we got straight to work. A trailer we dreaded unloading was beckoning. As the smaller items diminished and left a plethora of larger objects to be removed, Herman was offered a helping hand. "Awww, how cool" i thought, "My honey is making nice with the neighbors!" Herman paid this stranger for his kindness. One good deed deserves another. That night after dinner as the kids were preparing for bed, Herman took me by the hand, led me to our bedroom, closed the door behind us, and holding both of my hands, began jumping up and down! I thought he was losing it, but I knew it was the newfound excitement of this major step in our lives as a couple, as a family. So I, holding his hands, began jumping up and down with him...

THE LONGEST DAY

Not long after I was forced to endure the longest night, I was to suffer through the longest day. Social security cards, birth certificates, immunizations charts, report cards from the previous schools stating that each had been promoted, was ready. The kids were brushed, combed, and all washed up. Breakfast had been eaten, and all were hesitantly ready to go. Our 1st stop was the elementary school to enroll the girls. There was a load of paperwork x 2. It was here that I learned my children would be attending schools that required a uniform to be worn, so much for those cute back to school outfits. With all my t's crossed and i's dotted, I bid farewell to my little ladies. My next stop, middle school. This registration was very different. At the elementary we sat at a table in the library and I filled out individual packets. I thought this would be similar. The middle school registration was to take place in the gym. And instead of sitting at a table waiting to be called, this process was orchestrated through a number of stations. After that paperwork was complete, my son and I made our way to his homeroom, but not without getting slightly lost! After saying goodbye to my oldest and getting lost once more, I made my way out of the middle school, only to head back to pick the girls up at the release of their 1st day of school, and then back to pick up my son. What a day!!!

FALL

A LITTLE PIECE OF HOME

My mother came to visit. How cool is that? She brought with her, my stepdad and niece, which was a complete surprise. We had been counting down the weeks and were glad they had finally arrived. But no one told us that my niece would be in attendance. I was finishing up dinner when they pulled into the apartment complex; tilapia, salad, and grits. All enjoyed dinner and each other's company. The next day we had plans to go to Underground Atlanta. Watching my stepdad on the train was too hilarious for words. He kept asking, "Which stop is our stop?" Underground Atlanta was fun. My son got several compliments from the ladies, as usual! After the train ride back, we went to the J.C Penney Outlet my mother had been looking forward to going to, and in the end didn't even make a purchase, go figure. Sunday morning came all too fast. My parents and niece had to return to my hometown. Everyone said their goodbyes after breakfast and I was a little sad, still I was glad to have held if only for a short while, a little piece of home!

HEY... I THOUGHT THIS WAS SUPPOSED TO BE A HOUSEWARMING

A feast any woman would have been proud to present. Garden salad, fried tilapia, low country boil, Cajun style corn on the cob, rock shrimp alfredo, and a dessert tray of broken chocolate bars, sweet bread and cheese. During the preparation of this meal, all were in hyper help mode. My son and Herman did their share of helping out in the kitchen. I was ever grateful for that! I was beginning to get nervous as 6:30 approached. Why? Because i'm not what most would consider a 'social butterfly', 'antisocial' is more like it, thanks to my standoffish nature! 6:45 p.m., still no guests. The 1st knock came at 7. The guys, then another knock, and another... more guys! I was a little disappointed at first, but I quickly dismissed this notion. Besides, men love me! Cards, chess, and conversation, I'm practically one of them. The kids were pretty much in their own world and Herman seemed glad that so many of his male friends came to celebrate the new place with us. His cousin, a girl, did stop through, and I was glad, as I had been looking forward to meeting her for quite some time. All the guys got a good laugh at Herman's grade school photos and they were all in disbelief that I still owned vhs tapes... it's a vcr/dvd combo! Ok, stop laughing already! Herman thought it would be interesting to share with the guys an intriguing artifact from my past, a small, concealable handheld digital scale, an item attained from a previous life. Seemingly inconspicuous until all realized what it was. Their reactions were priceless. That within itself certainly placed me in their inner circle. The housewarming turned 'guy's night out' lasted well past midnight, with the man of the house knowing all too well, work was in the a.m.! Overall it was a good night, until, the last shot. I did my fair share of drinking throughout the night, preparing and mixing my own rum and cokes. Something told me not to do it, but I did it anyways! After drinking that shot of Bacardi 151° it was lights out.

HE'S SO EASY

He's so easy... to please that is! The ingredients; 1 tablespoon of butter, 3 golden pearl onions finely chopped and leftover chicken, diced. Butter melted, onions sautéed, add diced chicken, and sprinkle with black pepper. Toast two slices of white bread, light mayo. Spoon meat unto each slice, fold in half... walah! A quick after dinner, before bed snack. He thinks i'm a great cook, and I am, that and he's so easy to please!

OBSESSED

I can't remember who pointed it out, a box full of free books in the lobby of our local library. As usual, I was on the hunt for a Danielle Steele novel. Lo and behold I found one, but it was a title that I already owned, so I bypassed it. Then a curious title caught my eye, 'The Cove'. It did not have a flashy cover, but I know how deceiving looks can be. So I picked up this book of about 300 pages, read the prologue and decided to take this unassuming book home. I didn't intend to get so wrapped up in it, but from the 1st page I was hooked. Line by line, page by page, chapter by chapter, it just kept getting better! I could not, I repeat, I could not put it down. I read in the kitchen as I prepared dinner, I read while the children did homework, I read during dinner, I read in the bathroom, I read while the rest of the family watched a movie, I read in bed as the rest of the house slept! I only wanted to finish the chapter I was on when I lay down about midnight. But midnight soon turned into 4:30 a.m. I had to force myself to close the book. That 6:30 wakeup call was approaching fast. I continued to read throughout that next day. Herman must have thought me obsessed. He asked if I felt I could write a book of that nature. Just as good, yes! But fiction suspense is not exactly my genre! Me writing mystery... now that story would suck. I think I'll stick to poetry and creative nonfiction!!!

NOT ON THE KITCHEN FLOOR

The first time I saw him was during the housewarming. He was right outside our door on the stairs sitting near Herman and a friend. I guess they stepped out to escape the noise of many conversations taking place at once. I joined them on the balcony to ask if they needed anything. That is when I saw him. Ears erect, eyes shining, and the most beautiful coat! He was the biggest cat I had ever seen, a calico with markings that resembled that of an ocelot. I sat on the stairs and rubbed his fur, paying special attention to the spot under his chin, near his neck; cats love to be scratched here! A few nights later after that first feline encounter, he returned. This time we let him inside. He seemed pretty tame to us, not like some skittish wild thing. I opened a can of tuna, which the kitty happily devoured. After a bowl of water the kids played with him and began toying with the idea of keeping him. All decided he should have a name. Since I'm usually the one to name the pets, they looked to me for input. Koda or Kobe, were my suggestions. I preferred Koda. So of course they chose Kobe, so Kobe it was. I made plans to go by the leasing office to inform the rental agent of the newest member of our household. Also a trip to the vet was in order. But before I got the chance to, the cat began pacing near the front door. That was my cue that this was a cat that had no desire to be kept. He wanted out. The kids were sad. Herman opened the door, and the darndest thing, Kobe refused to go. He sauntered very cat like towards the kitchen, looking back as if he knew all eyes were upon him. Then he did it! Pissed all over my clean kitchen floor. All eyes were no longer watching him, as they were watching me to see my reaction. Horrified not because he had peed on the kitchen floor, but because I knew I was the one who was gonna have to clean it. I bleached the floor twice, after putting 'Kobe' out.

ARGUING OVER DISHES

No, there were not dishes between us, but there were dirty dishes in the sink, every cup and bowl, and all the silverware. So I rolled up my sleeves. This was done with much grumbling. Halfway through, I decide, the family can only use what's available! So I grabbed a stack of plates and relocated them. Herman laughed at the sight of what seemed to be perfectly logical to me! Needless to say, the sound of his laughter irritated the hell outta me in that moment. I dunno why... lack of sleep, my already present agitation, or maybe hunger. Whatever it was, I lost it. How dare he laugh at me, and I went off, much to his chagrin. He hates to disagree, let alone argue. Then to add insult to injury, he proceeds to grab every dish throughout the house and those in the refrigerator as well, so that I could wash those too. Wow! Unbelievable! Finally finished, now he wants to talk, and I don't wanna hear it. You think! But no matter how high I erect that wall, he always gets over. Not mad at him anymore, now I'm mad at myself for arguing over something as petty as dishes.

AN UNEXPECTED FRUSTRATION

Super excited, the fact that he proposed still thrills me. So naturally, I wanted to start putting on paper all of my fairytale wedding ideas. And they came fast and many. I would immerse myself in bridal magazines. I was dead set on using my favorite colors, pink and black. I knew who I wanted my bridesmaids to be, we had chosen the perfect song, and an awesome venue. You know the basic beginnings of a wonderful wedding. Then daydreams of a gown with detachable train came screeching to a halt. Seems my honey felt I was taking on way too much. With relocating the kids to Atlanta, finding a larger apartment, and summer nearing its end, he suggested I put wedding talk on pause until all was situated. But truth be told, Herman had visions of wedding planners dancing in his head. So, we moved into a beautiful apartment and the children had since bid ado to summer as a new school year began. Several weeks had passed without any mention of bridesmaids and bouquets, and then like a veil being lifted, I remembered! Well, actually it remembered me as I stumbled across a bridal magazine that had been overlooked during unpacking. And just like that, I was back! 4 tiered wedding cake or cupcakes, dj or band, photographer of videographer. Then the colors changed from hot pink, black, and white to blush pink, mint green, and buttercream. But my main concern, aside from the staggering rough draft guest list of about 300, was the feeling that I was the only one talking veils and tiaras! I tried to dismiss that minor frustration with a thought, that this was girl talk and perhaps my honey felt this was not his territory. But the more I attempted to piece the picture, the more frustrated I became. Sensing my agitation, Herman gave his valued opinion on a few dress styles I really liked. We talked venues and numbers. We compromised on a guest list that was much smaller and more intimate, not something he was thrilled about. Still, the sacrifice of his time was no small thing to me.

JUST RIGHT

Last night the honey slipped out momentarily. Even though I was in semi ill spirits he left with good intentions. By the time he returned the kids were in bed. As I sat on the couch attempting to gather my thoughts, he worked diligently in the kitchen preparing a treat. He emerged with a bowl of sliced pound cake with strawberries and cream Frappuccino ice cream in one hand and a glass of Moscato in the other. While he was out, he picked up a Redbox movie, 'Just Right'. I joked about my crush on Common, and he playfully threatened to cheat on me with Halle Berry! The tension that had built up over the course of a day began to dissipate as the remaining of our evening unfolded. I smiled to myself as I thought; he may not be perfect, but he's just right!!!

THE MIXOLOGIST

I dunno what movie we were watching but the guy behind the bar states, "I'm not a bartender, I'm a mixologist!" This has hence become Herman's at home title! I cook the meals and he mixes the drinks... now that sounds like a plan to me!

POETIC ASIDES

My beloved has given me a writing prompt. A poem. The catch? 5 lines, using the word 'tasty'...

HIS BODY
HIS LIPS
HIS MIND
HIS LOVE
TASTY

MIRROR IMAGE

UNSURE OF HOW THE REST OF THE WORLD SEES HIM
BUT HE'S BEAUTIFUL IN MY EYES!
HE IS PERFECT IN HIS IMPERFECTIONS
TO SEE HIM IS TO SEE MY OWN
REFLECTION

SOMETHING INCONSPICUOUS

Posting online, encouraging all the ladies to participate in breast cancer awareness, "Save the Tata's ladies!" During a self breast check, I noticed something inconspicuous under my left arm very near my breast. I had noticed this lump there sometime before, but had not given it much thought simply by choosing to ignore it. It was pretty forgotten until my fingertips played across it. Now what???

BEING TEASED, MERCILESSLY

This has definitely turned out to be a birthday to remember. It actually began 2 weeks before the day! I'm always super excited when the Scorpio moon is upon us. Posting fun facts on my Facebook profile, about this, my kick ass zodiac sign, was the way it started. Then commenced the teasing, the merciless, unashamed teasing. Herman! He got off early the Friday before my birthday. Coming through College Park after taking care of some business, we picked up one of his closest friends. They had plans to do a little birthday shopping that afternoon. He had been teasing me, now out actually getting the gift only heightened my anticipation. Needless to say, they took their sweet time. I was in the shower when he returned so I didn't get to sneak a peek at the bags or see where he hid them. Unlucky me. I was forced to wait, and be tortured another day!

A BIRTHDAY TO REMEMBER

A weekend filled with love, laughter, and life! What more could a girl ask for? I begged him all night as to a clue, what could it be? My gift... the torturous teasing continued. And then, he relented, reluctantly! He promised to give me my first gift at midnight, 12:00 a.m. the day before my birthday. I couldn't wait! Finally, ½ the cruel and unusual punishment was over. Carefully wrapped, and then unwrapped. How pretty! A silver toned necklace from one of my favorite stores, Icing! Suspended from the necklace was an array of charms. Each trinket embodied the symbol of amour! The Eiffel Tower, a key, a crystal studded heart, and a silver disc with the word 'Amour'. How pretty! Now I was really excited, I wondered what else my honey had in store for me. Upon waking up, Herman surprised me by asking if I wanted the other present! I thought he was joking. But he was very serious. He produced from the closet, a mocha colored Ed Hardy bag! I sat up in bed with outreached hands and wide eyes. As I made a move to get outta bed, Herman took a step back. Then he turned and ran out of the room, literally forcing me to chase him for my birthday gift! The bag was awesome and even more so as it was filled with a fragrance gift set! We spent the evening with his sister and her family. The grownups lounged around and the kids sang karaoke. Later that evening we enjoyed dinner out. Sunday, finally, my birthday, the weekend had been great. Birthday love from the kids was priceless! Handmade, heartfelt cards from each of them and a contract? Stating that they would be extra sweet for my birthday! Now there is something a girl could use. We attended church together and afterwards attended a baby shower. I gifted the mom to be with a very chic, pink, brown and white baby blanket, quilted by yours truly. Herman was excited to watch this blanket take form and once done, he bragged, blush! During the shower, I began to get a little stuffy. Oh no, I had been trying really hard not to get sick. Extra fluids, vitamin c, and the cooties still got me, and on this day of all days... oh no! I spent the remaining hours of my birthday sick in bed. As I blew my nose for the millionth time, I had to admit, it was for certain a birthday to remember.

3:30 A.M.

Can't sleep. Insomnia is not the guilty party. It's the Honey. He refuses to let me snooze. Up all night long like a couple of love struck teenagers, talking about everything and nothing in particular. Tickling each other, well, him tickling me! And although I'm delirious from a lack of sleep, I love our 3:30 a.m. sessions. Sleepily, I entangle myself in his embrace as 4 a.m. nears!

BE PREPARED

I'm on the living room floor stretching after a quick cardio. Herman is on the couch beside me. I hear a faint whirring sound. I threaten him that I better not smell a thing, I joke that he probably blew a hole in the seat. He looks at me dumbfounded. The noise does not fade. So I turn my momma ears on! The whir is followed by a low steady beep. I turn the television off so that I can hear better. It's louder now, he and I are up. I put my ear to our closed bedroom door. It's not the alarm clock. At the front door. Unlatched, unbolted, door open. Smoke is everywhere. My neighbors are coming out of their apartments. The smoldering cloud is rising from downstairs. Herman is back in the house. In two steps and 2 quick flicks of his wrist, he is down the hall and the kid's room doors fly open. "Get up, put your shoes on, and grab your blankets!" He is saying. And the kids are up and out. My amiga across the veranda is steps behind her esposo, he has la bebe all bundled up. In my amiga's hand is a folder. I think good idea. Grab the envelope with the kid's birth certificates, social security cards, and immunization records! And where are my keys and wallet? None are found so I settle for my brown bag, the one with my stories, poetry, blog entries and jump drive. Downstairs it's chaos, everybody trying to figure out what's going on. It seems the apartment directly below us caught afire. The little boy, a younger friend of my son's, was at home with his grandmother, apparently asleep when he heard her cry for help. It's all he remembers, the fear in her voice and the smoke. Atlanta's finest came to the rescue. Fire fighters, police officers and emergency workers were on the scene in the matter of minutes. Luckily for building 400, it was a small fire contained in the confines of our neighbor's kitchen. I'm just glad it did not turn into a much larger disaster. Glad we were all prepared.

HERMAN'S DREAM

He says we were out shopping. My hair was long and flowy. He was holding a baby boy and I was holding the hand of a little girl. Awww, how sweet? To have more children together. To strengthen the bond that already cements our family in love with a baby! Now I'm thinking of baby names, and that in turn has my cycle all off whack. Herman is so funny. He talks about 'getting me knocked up!' who says that? This really isn't 1915! After the wedding we intend to extend the Jackson-Taylor family. A son to carry his father's namesake, a daughter to princess! But for now, dreams of babies are all we can have. Researching the procedure and costs to have my tubal ligation reversed. It seemed like a good idea at the time. But now as I look at my biologically childless, husband to be, there is nothing I want to give him more! He assures me that even if this does not come to pass it in no way changes his love for me. He loves 'our' children, and once they are grown and gone, I'll still be his baby.

SETTING A DATE

I really do have my heart set on a wedding in the spring! What little girl doesn't? I'm able to squeeze a word in edgewise about the wedding on occasion. But truthfully, it's not as discussed as I would like for it to be, which is somewhat unsettling. I have a slight idea as to a few things he likes, and he has a general overview as to the things I prefer. But what of the things we don't agree on? There really should be some conversing going on, a little communication please! Could we at least set a date to this self planned fiasco?

THROWING IN THE TOWEL

I regretfully sit down to write, that today is not a good day! Well, not anymore. I spoke with his sister this a.m. and she had me inspired, motivated, and in good spirits. After our conversation I decided to write a few random thoughts on sticky notes. When I was done, I placed each strategically on the bathroom mirror so that Herman would see them when he came home! The general tone of the notes was easy and mellow, nothing too loud. I just wanted him to know how I felt about certain aspects of our impending wedding. Seems the point I was trying to make, sadly, eluded him. I only wished we did not have to put so much expense into the details of our day. It's more important to me, our union. I could care less whom we impress. But it seems to me he is all about the dollar sign sometimes. I think he subconsciously feels the extravagance of the ceremony and reception is somehow attached to his status. So I sit here, aggravated, frustrated; feeling like throwing the towel in. Wayne's 'The Carter III; Comfortable' loud in my ear to match my mood... and I write. The pen assaults paper with each flick of my wrist. Funny, the pressure he's complaining about right now is the same pressure that led me to Atlanta, the same pressure that turned me into some weird persistent chic. It's the same pressure that led to a proposal and a yes... towel on the ground!

I LOVE YOU

Sensing my ill mood, he pulled the ear buds from their resting place and Wayne's words became incoherent. No! "Just let me be, let me stew in this funk you've placed me in, dammit!" Furious, he refuses to let me be angry. His hands at my waist pulling me out of my seat, snatching me back to reality. I grudgingly resist. I don't wanna. Yeah I'm being a brat in this moment. Still he wouldn't give an inch. I comply, as if I have a choice. Steered to our bathroom, he forces me to look up. There on the mirror before me, 5 blue sticky notes, each whispering "I love you". Now how can I be mad at that? A smile escapes my lips and I hug him. He breathes into my neck, April 2, 2011.

<u>TOO WEIRD</u>

My kids think I'm so weird! They are wondering why I left stickys all over the bathroom mirror, as opposed to just talking. Sure I could do that. But I much prefer to do things differently at times. To expectedly do the unexpected, because it's expected of me. Weird huh?

APRIL 2, 2011

Still in shock! After much anticipation and plenty of debate, a date has been set! I must confess, I was in complete disbelief. Now I'm beginning to feel like this is really gonna happen. It's hard to believe, but in my excitement I didn't call, text, or post my good news. I wanted to revel in its glow before sharing with the world. The next day of course, it was time to share this treasured date. April 2, 2011! My honey and his sister were thrilled, as were my parents. With passing this information along, minor details came into play. Two options lay on the table. Option A & Option B. Option A, Herman's choice, consists of a beautiful, extravagant, costly wedding, reception and honeymoon. Option B, my choice, entails a small, quaint, and just as beautiful, more intimate ceremony; a reception tailored to suit our combined tastes, and a honeymoon that would require some creative planning! But I suppose those details will untangle themselves. We have a date!

THE GOOD, THE BAD, THE BUTTON

I picked it up several weeks ago at a Stonecrest Mall outing. When I saw it, I had to have it; a novelty button about 3 inches around, that boasted "Kiss the Bride" in my two favorite colors, pink & black. A set of hot lips with diamond accent for that extra bling! So cute... so chic... so me! After purchasing the button I displayed it in a clear sheet protector, claiming I would wear it after the fact of the matter. You know. Walk down the aisle, exchange vows, say I do, kiss, all that mushy stuff. Then we set a date, finally, and I got to itching. I wanted to wear my button. But would it be politically incorrect? So the detective in me went immediately to work. The American Heritage 4th edition dictionary states that a bride is a woman recently married or about to be married. So with this knowledge, I pulled said button from its humble display, vowing to wear it every day until the day I say "I do". I pinned it proudly upon my breast the day we began our Thanksgiving vacation. A 4 hour drive and we were back in my hometown. The first to spot my pretty little button was my aunt. And it began. She called for my uncle. His kiss was the 1st but not the last. Kisses that followed were endured from another uncle who smelled of whiskey, a cousin that had been smoking, a not so little baby brother, and a few male friends. Herman was a good sport. I'm just glad my path did not cross with that of any strangers during our visit. On that last day, I noticed that the button, not the bride had lost its mojo. Then I discovered that all the kisses my cheek had endured had rubbed the letters off of my once cute button. The thought occurred to purchase another. Nah!!!

<u>REHABILITATED</u>

Herman, you have rehabilitated my soul. Because of you, my heart has been healed. Never have I felt this way about another and it leaves me wondering why now? Why now does my heart choose to love? I believe with every ounce of my being, that you, not I, am the better half. Seeing me for the frail creature I was, not the woman you stand before, stronger today as wounds heal in your love. Thank you for hearing my voice and bringing forth laughter. Even in silence, the bond between us is beautiful, brash, and bold. An incomplete spirit, now whole. My mended heart, your own. Thank you for rehabilitating my soul. I love you.
I believe I just wrote my vows!

WINTER

TROUBLE IN PARADISE

A phone call really would have been nice. Off early at noon to take care of the truck. Another tire! Yet it's well after 4 when you come walking through the door. Yes, the elephant ring you picked up for me is very pretty. Why the gift? What did you do wrong? I guess it's the cynic in me that finds a way to distrust the silver lining. Once you've been hurt, you learn to put your guard up. But really, the need is irrelevant with him. I have never been given a reason to doubt. And I guess it truly is time to let past hurts go. Still, when he walks in, I can't resist the urge to put up a little fight. Amidst my rambling, his sister's words rang loud in my ear, "The closer you get to saying I do, the more it will seem you are arguing over everything and nothing". So the seeming trouble in paradise is all a mirage? What a relief!

NOT LOSING SIGHT

With the much needed, much appreciated help of Herman's sister, I felt like everything was under control. Then a text and a call. Seems he has a cousin that would like to meet with me, to offer ummmmmmmmm, advice? Input? Ideas... oh! 'Ideas' Herman says. Everyone is excited about our big day and we should be psyched that others are interested in helping. It's just that I'm not accustomed to so much assistance. Honestly, I was prepared to go it alone. We meet on a Sunday. I have decided to take a platter of silent sandwiches. If an 'idea' doesn't quite suit my taste, I plan to daintily pick up one of these delectable morsels, chew on it, and nothing more! But who knows, perhaps I will get a few good 'ideas' or some much needed information. If all else fails, I've been advised by my team mate to not lose sight of the wedding we envision!

HOW TO BECOME A BRIDE (OR GROOM): LOOKING FOR THE PERFECT MATE

Looking for the perfect mate is much like deep sea fishing! Or so I've heard. Since I'm not one with nature, it's difficult for me to grasp this analogy. So I will compare it to, lets say, shopping for shoes, something most can relate to. So, lets try it again... Looking for the perfect mate is much like shopping for the perfect pair of shoes. It is in the sense that not just any shoe will do. The first fit is usually not the best fit. And just because they look good on display does not mean they're the pair for you. They should complement you and stand out, all in the same breath, just as the perfect mate should!

OOH LA LA

Out shoe shopping with the sister in law to be. For some reason the best shoes always come in size 8 ½. Why? I've really got my eyes open for the perfect pair of size 10's! It just so happens I did spot a few pair that I fancied. But I didn't want to limit my options, so I continued to look. Always a softie for a sale, the clearance rack called out to me. I found the most awesome pumps. A pretty pair of 3 inch heels, black and white pin stripes, peep toe, with a bow across the front. Beyond pretty, magnifique. They looked like they belonged to a Parisian model and I wanted them. I grabbed the box and deciding to forgo checking the size, I prayed to the shoe fairy. "Please let it fit, please let it fit!" Too small. Did she not hear me? My shoe shopping partner having spied the mishap picks up the shoe's mate, slides it onto her foot in a Cinderella moment, and it fit. The story of my life. Looking for a size 10 when all I can find is an 8 ½!

SMOKE IN THE CITY

Oh what a day! It all started before we even left the parking lot. Girls in tow, we prepared to make the 0.5 mile drive to school. As usual they were bickering about nothing, girls! I put the truck into reverse, checked the mirror, and proceeded to back into the parking lot. Then I saw her, the lady in the mirror. She was walking through the parking lot that also serves as a makeshift sidewalk. I swear I must have been mere inches from hitting her! What a way to start my day. In a shaken state of mind, I commence to drop the girls off. While waiting at the red light I hear something like a balloon burst. Then came the smoke, thick white smoke that emitted from beneath the hood on the passenger side. Mind you, I'm pretty savvy in a number of things to a certain degree, but this was out of my league! I made it home, thank goodness it's only a short drive. Once upstairs, my son is informed of the situation. He, new to the teenage years is an expert in all things, so he thinks! He inspects under the hood and gives his 'expert' opinion. "Radiator, mama." he exclaims. I shrug. Maybe. A quick text between the sis and I and she suggests checking the water level and adding more if necessary. Ok, that done, oh no! The water leaked out, but not from the radiator. It seemed to be running off from another location. Where? I don't know. I'm no pep boy. I simply prayed Jade, oh Jade is our truck, anywho, I just hoped she would make it through the day. I dropped my son off at school. Thankfully the trip was uneventful. After a few hours I thought I'd try my luck, but it proved disastrous. Halfway to my destination, Jade decided to bless the city once more. This time the smoke was worse. I allowed her a time out to cool down, and we were back at it again. I had to pick the kids up! Fingers, eyes, and toes crossed. Elementary... check. Middle school... check. Home... crickets chirp! The truck started and died in the middle of the school parking lot. To add insult to injury, it began to rain. Great! Knee deep in flood water, Jade in neutral, my son and I pushed until the truck was clear of traffic. Praying and cranking, praying and cranking. The engine refused to turn over. What luck, stuck! Called up the sis, and lo and behold, she arrives, I twist the key in the ignition, Jade cranks. Unbelievable!

A LABOR OF LOVE

The cost of wedding stationary v/s my creative ability. Handcrafted engagement announcements it is! It has truly been a labor of love. But every ribbon, bow and super glued finger has been so worth it.

THE SKY IS THE LIMIT

Putting the specifics of our special day in black in white has not occurred without much compromise. Not only are hearts and minds required to meet at some common ground, so are ideas. We have decided against the traditional wedding cake and opted for tiers of cupcakes instead. Besides, one too many a horror story is heard of guests not getting a slice of cake. That and I, having done some research, have discovered that the groom's cake was initially intended for the 'wedding cake', so nix the 4 tiered expectancy. We are however going to keep with today's tradition of the groom's cake, chocolate of course! Silks for the bouquets and live for the boutonnieres. Photographer or videographer? That one is still up for debate. Each component as we decide is being put to a budget. I have a pretty clear idea of what we can and can't afford. My ideal wedding is pretty, chic, intimate, and won't clean out the bank! Herman however, with his big dreams, resides in the clouds. And where a budget is concerned, the sky is the limit! I too have big dreams, but my feet are firmly planted on the ground as I attempt to be realistic. Can you meet me half way? Shall we meet at the horizon?

THAT WENT WELL

I met with his sister and cousin today, and contrary to my initial feelings, the meeting went rather well. Having assisted brides to be before me, his cousin was curious to know if we were on the right track. She offered useful information. The three of us huddled and accomplished much in the conversation. Herman was present as well, offering his input when and where needed. I was reminded of a few things such as getting information of the nearest hotel and something I had not considered, requesting shuttle service to and from the ceremony/reception site. Amidst the conversation I had the idea that it would be really cool and cost efficient to distribute save the dates at our engagement party, brilliant! I'm really glad I didn't walk into the house close minded. I'm always game for a few good ideas!

BRIDE-A-SAURUS

Herman spent the day with his big sister. They made a trip to David's Bridal to situate the apparel finances. He was horrified to learn that the shoes I chose to wear beneath my gown were pink, watermelon to be exact. He called to inquire about this, I confirmed. No one would see the shoes. I even contemplated heels of a cornflower hue, for my something blue. But pink is one of my favorite colors, that and black, so naturally when I saw the watermelon heels I had found my shoe. With my confirmation, Herman informs me that he will be wearing tangerine shoes, as if! He only wished to get a rise out of me. He succeeded. In his success, my skin turned a greenish tint. Scales surfaced. Spikes formed where hair once had been. A tail, claws, and carnivorous teeth... behold the bride-a-saurus! Grrrrr! My day. My feet. My shoes. Pink! Pink! Pink!

THAT COULD BE PRETTY

The black and white engagement invites has really got me reconsidering the colors of our wedding. Changed several times already; black and hot pink, my faves... lime green, I dunno what I was thinking... ivory and tangerine, although the dress I love, love, love is white. How about tangerine, black, and white? I have been instructed per my future husband that this is the last change. He put his foot down and I put my finger to my temple in thought mode. Hmmmm, blue and yellow is really pretty...

A BLACK AND WHITE AND RED LITTLE NUMBER

Looking for the perfect engagement party outfit. The theme of the evening, formal. A black and white, tie optional event. I swear we checked every shop, mall, and store. I did find a few cute dresses and of course more awesome heels I vowed to revisit! Last stop, a clothing boutique in College Park. There were some nice dresses at the front of the shop, but I'm a sucker for a sale, so I hit the clearance racks! Black and white, with a hint of something that pops to set me apart from the crowd. Besides, it's all about me, I mean us, wink! Sifting through throngs of hangers, I found exactly what I was looking for! A black leather skirt, how perfect. To complete the look, a white camisole and red blouse with a wide, black patent leather belt, and a pair of large black hoops. Sexy! Now all I needed were those heels i'd been dying for. A pair of black and white zebra striped pumps with red heels! Next stop... shoes!

NOT CHEAP... CONSCIOUS

Just because I prefer not to go into debt, does not make me cheap. So what? I'm aware of price tags and dollar signs. This makes me conscious. And a conscious bride makes for a good wife! $2,000.00 dress my ass, pardon the language. I'll take the one for $500 Alex!

A PASSING THOUGHT

A passing yet hilarious thought. In a few short months
Herman will officially be Mr. Katandra!

4 EXTRA MONTHS

4 extra months... of preparation that is! We planned so carefully the date of our big day, taking into consideration everyone's work and school schedules. April 2nd, the weekend before spring break would be perfect as the children would be out of school. Taking into account the weather and deciding the bridal attire around the season, we sought and found the perfect location to host our special day. I call to reserve the date only to learn they are booked solid until July 31, 2011. Oh my wow! Hyperventilate! Phone in hand, I text a friend who informs me that it's not the end of the world. She reminds me to breathe and regroup! Deep breath in, deep breath out, okay. I can make July 31st work for us! After all, it's not about the date, it's about the promise. Besides, this gives us 4 extra months... to prepare.

PROPER ETTIQQUETE

Hey, did I spell that correctly? Oh well! Whatever! So I've been informed that it is proper etiquette for the bride and groom to foot the bill for the engagement party! Or is it the bride's family? Wait, maybe it's the groom's family that is supposed to pay? In any case it's not economically smart. Directly following Christmas, New Year's Day was fast approaching. I don't know about anyone else's household, but most don't exactly have the money to throw around a mere week after Christmas. Putting the invites together, I didn't give much thought as to who was 'supposed' to pay. Who follows etiquette anymore, anyways?

PASSPORTS

It's been up for debate! Where shall we honeymoon? Cruises and Island vacations are becoming so common day. Not that we've indulged in either, still we would like to stay away from the beaten path. My Honey has been thumbing through this magazine his sister thought he would like, and he does! It's full of destination weddings and honeymoon spots. I've asked Herman to dog-ear the pages of those locations that interest him most. A 200 page magazine has been dog-eared 150 times. Ok... now to eliminate 149! I thumb through his selections and I'm seeing a lot of choices referenced at Mexico, one location in particular that has caught my eye, Puerto Vallarta Mexico. And I'm thinking, perfect! Who doesn't love a good siesta after a fiesta? Mexico it is. I'm assuming this means airfare, and something that never dawned on me, passports are in order. But why? Isn't Mexico a part of North America? I'm confused, but okay. Passports it is!

DRINKING ALONE

I'll be the first to admit to having slight trust issues. This problem that stems from the past is not something I'm proud of. Just the same, I own it! A few weeks ago Herman spotted the jacket he wanted last winter but regretfully did not get. Me being the loving fiancé' that I am, encouraged him to purchase it this time. After all, he deserves it. He does so much for all of us. So the week before Christmas I gave free reign! Preferring to be close to him at all times, yet knowing I really need to learn to let go! If you love him, you'll trust him... right? Right! After a few kisses, with key in hand, he bound down two flights of stairs and proceeded to his destination. I did pretty good for the first hour, not noticing as the minutes went by. This was a good thing. But at precisely one hour, as if an alarm went off inside of me, I noticed the time. The first five minutes were pure torture. I tried to convince myself not to call, but I was too weak, I caved! I just had to hear his voice. He answered, sounding newly refreshed and as handsome as ever. Relief! Kinda, to calm down what remained of jittery nerves, I poured my third glass of Moscato Spumante and sank into a warm bath.

BEST CHRISTMAS EVER

The tree and all the ornaments waited patiently in a quiet corner in the living room of our first apartment. This too would be another first. Birthdays and holidays shared, but this, our first Christmas was sure to be extra special. It was the kids 1st Christmas in the city. Having spent all previous Christmases in our hometown, they initially frowned at the idea of spending this very sacred holiday away from 'home'. But this was home now. The weekend that kicked off their holiday vacation they began to get extra excited. We put the tree up after rearranging the furniture. The kids took turns hanging the ornaments. I smiled at memories from years gone as they hung ornaments their once smaller hands made. With the tree all dolled up, she was missing one thing, the star! We awaited Herman's arrival so that he could do the honors. He and I thought we'd get a rise outta the kids by putting nameless gifts under the tree. This drove the kids insane. Of course as the gifts continued to accumulate, we labeled them, much to the relief of 3 anxious children. As the days passed the holiday spirit persistently filled our cozy apartment. Stocking stuffers were opened Christmas Eve day and that night we joined his sister's family and friends for dinner. The kids were glad for an early exchange of gifts. That night while the kids slept peacefully in their beds Herman and I settled in on the living room floor to watch a movie. Morning came like a thief without warning. The kids were awake. It was Christmas. They tore into their gifts, their voices enthusiastic, and each facial expression priceless. Herman enjoyed his gifts. And then it was my turn. Days before I stood in front of the tree wondering what was in each box Herman had wrapped and labeled 'Kat'. When no one was looking I even picked up one very heavy gift. I was as eager as the children. Herman placed the first gift in my hand. I unwrapped it slowly, deliberately not ripping into the pretty paper. The house was in a moment of suspense. Color hit my eye... a shade of my favorite color, pink... fuchsia! A wool petticoat; very clean, classic, and chic! Next was a very heavy box, the same one I had secretly lifted a few days before. It was now in my possession, I tore into the wrapping paper this time... a laptop!!! Not a netbook, a 15" laptop! This just keeps getting better, touched, I'm on the brink of tears. A package of printer paper unwrapped prompts a, "Is there a printer under there?" Wow. An office complete, everything I need to continue this literary journey. The icing on the cake to an already perfect Christmas, snow! Herman and the kids crunched their way across the living room floor, through the once lovely now tattered wrapping paper, and they made their way outside to enjoy the winter weather. I stayed inside, relishing this most awesome of moments, burning a memory! Friends, family, food, presents, love, laughter, life. This has been the best Christmas ever.

1-1-11

The kids had us singing karaoke and playing games. What better way to bring in the New Year? Herman and I celebrated with a bottle of Moscato Spumante champagne, my new fave to date. As always the kids watched in anticipation from a distance, the popping of the cork. My brother and his family had arrived and joined us as we toasted a new year! With morning, came my mother and cousin. Accompanying her was an armful of, yep you guessed it, more gifts! It was Christmas again for the children. 1-1-11 was a very busy day. It's always busy when family comes to visit, everyone with their own agendas, attempting to meet in the middle. My only m.o was to get through the day so that we could get to the night. Engagement party? Yes, engagement party! At the last minute, I decided against the black and white and red little number, opting instead for the classic little black dress. My honey donned a pair of black slacks, a crisp white shirt, and red tie. Before stepping out, I affixed our 'bride' & 'groom to be' pins. A few photos snapped with the family, jackets on and we were en route to our favorite 'hangout' restaurant, LaFiesta. Weeks prior to this special event, we met with the owner. She was glad to reserve a portion of the bar for our party. It was great, a black and white tie optional event. I was grateful to be surrounded by our family and a few of our closest friends. The food was great and the music was good. My favorite part of the night was the laughter that was shared as well as the well wishes that were bestowed upon the soon to be married couple.

OFF TO A GOOD START

My mother and Herman attended church Sunday morning. The rest of the family kinda lounged around at home. Tired from a night of partying, I only wished to relax and reflect on our amazing engagement party. When they returned, we prepared to say our goodbyes. A 4 hour drive awaited the crew from my hometown. They had made a special trip just for Herman and I, stating that they would not have missed it for the world. As we bid each other farewell and promised to see each other soon, Herman pointed out a hawk overhead. It was joined by another. I had never seen anything like it before. As I looked into the sky at the beautiful birds flying directly above, I hugged Herman and thought to myself, "We're off to a good start!"

SNOWED IN

Crazy weather we're having! It's snowing again 2 weeks after the New Year has begun. I'm so not used to this. My hometown is snugly located an hour away from Savannah GA. The air is cool there this time of year. But I'm freezing my buns off in Atlanta. Adding insult to injury, here comes the snow! Now the weather forecaster is announcing a snow day. I'm thinking okay, they will resume their school week on Tuesday as opposed to Monday, no big deal! Then Tuesday, Wednesday, a whole week. This is the worst! It's like being stranded with somewhere to go and no way to get there. Stranded, not on some desolate, remote, forsaken island... but at home with 3 children who seem to be growing more impatient with every passing moment. I'm on the brink of insanity! "Snow, snow, go away, so I can go outside and play!" Wow, really? I'm afraid I have a touch of cabin fever, aaaaaaagh.

AND ANOTHER ONE

What are the odds of me expanding the bridal party? I'd say very. I have asked a very close friend of mine if she would do me the honors of being my third bridesmaid. She has happily accepted, transforming the dynamic duo into 'Las Tres Mejor Chicas', the three best girls. No old 'maids' here! Herman and I have decided against the traditional titles of best man and maid/matron of honor. Feeling that each is just as important in our lives as is the next; loving them differently but with the same, exact amount of love! Now that she's in, I can't imagine my day without my P.I.C (Partner In Crime). Always just a phone call away. Cool, calm, and collected is this chica. The bridal party now consists of; 1 bride & groom, 2 flower girls, 2 jr. Brides, Tres Mejor Chicas, 1 ring bearer & 1 jr. Groom, + 5 best men = 16! I just had to go and add another one but I'm most certainly glad that I did!

MY BESTIE

The most awesome, kick ass chica I know. Well actually she is quiet and mild tempered but her personality is amazing. So naturally she is one of 'Las Tres Mejor Chicas'. I met her via the workplace about 5 years ago. Odd enough we became friends despite our only commonality at that time which was the acquaintances that worked alongside us. She remembered that I had children and invited us to her niece's birthday party back in 2006. A friendship was planted. As days, weeks, months, and years changed, so did our occupations. Friends temporarily lost contact with one another. Then the weirdest thing, our paths crossed once more in the unlikeliest of places, she was working at the school my children were attending. The friendship sprouted and blossomed. Closer than close, when her own children were born, she blessed me with the honors of being their godmother. She is a cool, confidant and amazing amiga. She is my bestie.

BRIDESMAIDZILLA

"Well I don't know if I like this dress style... They don't have it in my size... Is it gonna be long enough... I'm not really loving the 1 inch heel, I prefer 3..." roar, roar, roar! We have an opinionated (out of love) control freak bridesmaid in our midst. And it's not bothering me one bit. I'm trying not to lose it every time I get the urge to change something. Every minor detail directly linked to the next, tweaking one little element truly does affect the whole scheme. The last thing I need is those particulars weighing heavy on me coincidentally with keeping track of Las Chicas and their duties. Since they are all equal in stature, I never got around to divvying up the responsibilities. But like I said, it's cool. This chica keeps the trio in check and I'm glad for it! The big sister I never had, family just the same. Xoxoxoxo at her for always having my back, even if she is a Bridesmaidzilla!

NO THEME

I know a lot of brides are going the color coordinated route, but who says you have to abide by such a stuffy standard. I intend to break the mold that has been preset. Our engagement invitations were a classic black and white template, with fancy script, ribbons and bows... they were very formal, for quite the informal soiree. At current, I'm working on our save the dates. {Note to self: when to send out?} This piece of the wedding stationary puzzle is fun and quirky, quite like the soon to be couple at times. Three black and white, photo booth type pictures have been strategically arranged, tangerine (orange) lettering will complete the look. The ceremony invitation style that has been decided is contemporary chic; our engagement photo behind a translucent layer that has the invite wording, topped with a pretty satin bow, whose color has yet to be determined. That leaves programs, reception seating cards, announcements, and thank you notes. Each piece of the stationary puzzle different having no particular theme, and each with its own unexpectedly artistic twist! I'm loving this 'no theme' thing!

FUCHSIA TOO

Every recipe should have a secret ingredient! The wedding colors have been set in stone, so says my husband to be! Black, white, and tangerine. But the more I look the more I'm seeing the many shades of orange aside from tangerine; peach, mango, apricot, and papaya; each color just as pretty as its cousin. I've noticed certain hue variations border on being pink. That has got me reconsidering the color scheme. I can just see it. A bouquet of tangerine and fuchsia Casablanca Lilies!!!

POP CHAMPAGNE

Or wine, it's all the same thing to me. I attempted to decork a bottle of chardonnay. Unsuccessfully at first, I might add. I suppose watching it being done and actually doing it aren't exactly the same. I swear i've seen Herman perform this ritual on many occasion with his beloved Moscato. Cork screw in one hand, bottle in the other, laughingly mocking my ignorance. I had no idea where to even start. Do I try, try, and try again until I'm successful or do I just wait until the honey arrives. My lunch waiting on the table pressed me on. Much to the reward of my persistence, the cork surrendered to my efforts. Alas, lunch served with chardonnay.

IT'S QUIET

A little too quiet. The kids are back at school after a week of 'snow days'. Thank goodness for that. I was beginning to go loony, cooped up in the house all day every day for 10 days straight, that's enough to make a bald man sprout grey hair. In the absence of the pitter-patter of little feet x 3, I made plans to host a special mommy luncheon. I was really looking forward to spending the evening with my, I mean his sister. But the universe spoke and plans have been since delayed. The culprit? The truck? Again? Yep. It's always the truck! Now I'm stuck at home forced to eat lunch alone. Today's special Madame... our house tuna salad, leafy greens and a side of buttercrisp crackers, served with a 2009 chardonnay, exquisite.

P.s I love a good recipe...

House Tuna Salad
- 1- 12 oz. can chunk white albacore tuna
* ¼ cup ranch dressing
* A handful of diced celery
* Salt, pepper, and paprika to taste

Mix all ingredients in medium bowl. Serve with crackers. Enjoy!

PROJECT HUSH HUSH

Plans for Herman's 30th birthday are underway. A theme has been decided and details are being discussed. I'm not at liberty to disclose any information at this time in reference to Project Hush Hush, as I've been sworn to secrecy. Parties involved are afraid the plans will be compromised if we breathe a word! There will not be a breach in security.

IDEALISTIC ^{V/S} REALSTIC

A budget has been written, in black ink and plain language. Compiling the costs was easy. The hard part is compromising! Whereas one list now exists, two has emerged. We're calling them the 'Idealistic ^{v/s} Realistic' lists! It's ideal to host an intricate garden ceremony, to showcase ice sculptures as reception centerpieces and to honeymoon in Paris. But realistically speaking, these things seem extreme. Are we not still in a recession? The idealistic budget which consists of Herman's idealisms totals in at $15,000. The realistic budget, inspired by yours truly, totals in at $5,000. Two very different lists, two very different opinions, two very different visions. Now to negotiate. I figure if he and I could compromise, come to some sort of agreement, possibly marrying idealistic components in a realistic manner then our wedding day will be amazing.

DREAMING OF RINGS (BLING, BLING PART 1)

Okay so I'm daydreaming of rings. And not your average, typical, everyday ring either. I've stressed so many times that I'm not interested in a solitaire. If you've seen one diamond, you've seen em all. I am, however, partial to princess cut. Allergic to white gold, platinum is a little pricey and yellow gold is not really my thing. Honestly, opting for sterling silver seems weird. A previous visit to the jeweler proved to be beyond comical. Immediately, Herman went into character! He wanted the blingest ring they had. The sales associate must have thought him funny. She doubled over in laughter at the description he gave her as to what he was looking for. "Bling, bling, bling!" I didn't particularly see anything that I was wild about. But we did gather some pertinent information. Ring sizes, his and mine, 8 ½ and 9 ½! Now I'm fantasizing of a ring, or should I say 'bling'. One particular very specific ring. A wide band at least ½ inch in width, silver tone, sparkly, sexy. A paisley design wraps around the band in my little daydream, and the whole ring looks like it's been dipped in diamond dust... bling, bling, bling!

'THE' DRESS

After much looking and no luck, I believe I found the one. Not listed with the more popular styles, when given the online dress identification number, the saleslady exclaimed she had never seen it. But when I saw it I knew. Instantly. It was 'the' dress. At a whopping $1,500.00 less than the dress I thought was decided upon. This one was a more spectacular, more dramatic, more 'me' dress. The texture of the material, a buttery silk, side rouching at one waist, strapless, adorned with pearls and crystals, impeccable white, perfection! This time I was not looking for the confirmation in anyone else's eyes aside from my own, and I loved not only the way I looked in it, but the way I felt. I was a Princess on my way to become Queen. In that feeling I knew that this was 'the' dress.

SECRET FITTING

I really am thinking of going alone to try on a dress I saw online. Why after the fact that I've found my dream dress? Because I am doing my best to keep all costs within my realistic budget. I just don't feel comfortable spending so much on a single day. I mean, one must continue to live once this day is done. The more this realization dawns on me, the more I have the urge to get a more cost friendly dress. I don't know if this secret fitting is gonna come to pass, because I really do love my dress... but it sure is tempting!

I GOT MY SHOES

Store after store and still nothing, then like a prayer being heard, I found them. A pretty pair of low heels, size 10... thank you fairy shoe mother! I was in a bit of a funk when the sister in law to be suggested we go shoe shopping, claiming this would lighten my mood. Of course I ran into the usual suspects, size 8 ½'s curse you! A pair of pretty pumps caught my eye, but they turned out to be all wrong. Wrong width (narrow), wrong length (9 ½), wrong color (ruby red), and the wrong height (4 inches)! Just all wrong. The worst part was the uneasiness I felt as my weight shifted on the ultra-skinny heels. At $80.00, a bride to be on a realistic budget continued her search. Back at the same shoe store that housed the black, white and red zebra pumps I coveted, the assistance ran her sales pitch by me and I ran my specifics by her. Very particular about what I was looking for, I doubted very seriously I'd find my dream shoe or even come close. She produced several pair, but each only 80% fit the bill. It was a long shot in the dark, a stretch at its greatest, one more pair that might be exactly what I was looking for. As she disappeared behind a wall of shoes I doubted my search was over. Then she emerged with the most awesome pair of 2 inch size 10 heels color...?

TWO VEILS AND A TIARA

They're right you know! Once you've found 'the' dress, you should just stop looking. I guess I didn't get the memo. Every time I saw another dress the mental picture I had painted, changed. Still not sure as to the way I'm gonna wear my hair. But I certainly am playing with the idea of hair adornments; bird cage, blusher, fingertip, and cathedral veils, flowers, feathers and tiaras. I'm in love with the birdcage veil look, but trying it on, it did not love me back. I like the idea of flowers & feathers. It's so chic! But would that require me to wear my hair pulled into a ponytail? Then we have the veils, none of which I really like. I mean, they're pretty on other brides! I just don't think a veil is for me. It reminds me of bug screens used in the jungle or the veil of death they would lay atop a beloved queen while the kingdom mourned. It just wasn't my thing. So why am I wearing two then? Because they look amazing, accentuating my face and adding drama to my dress, two veils; one blusher and one cathedral, both white with intricate details at a scalloped edge... and a tiara!

FREEZE FRAME

Have you ever felt like you were at a place in your life where you knowingly stood on the brink of greatness, like something amazing is about to happen? Well I'm there! Standing in the midst of dresses, shoes, veils, and tiaras; there is a hint of something more! I'm loving the feeling. I'm gonna freeze frame this moment in time!

CRAZY IN LOVE

I've always been! It seems as if Herman has been bitten by the bug as well. He has spotted me pouting about something silly, and in true Herman form, he just won't let me be. The shower warm and the force of the water pulsating gently on my body, I hear the bathroom door creak open. I ignore it. The next thing I know, there he is, standing in the shower fully clothed! I'm laughing hysterically at his madness. As he pulls my wet body near I can see the love in his eyes and I know he too is crazy in love!

A DAY EARLY

I just received confirmation that our wedding date has been changed, again, bumped up a day early. After weeks of trying to contact the site coordinator to no avail, we began entertaining the thought that our dream locale was not gonna be in the big scheme of things. His sister was the first to learn of the place, and once Herman online searched it, his mind was made up. There was no persuading him to even think of another location. So of course his heart was broken at the idea of his not so perfect wedding. Then finally, some results! His sister spoke with the site coordinator and solidified the confirmation. Our ceremony and reception are to be held at a venue in Statesboro GA. Having spoken to the lady myself prior to the confirmation, I was under the impression that our deadline to pay the deposit to hold said grounds was fast approaching. I was also misunderstood in believing this place was booked until Sunday July, 31st. A Sunday wedding? This struck me as odd, but I played into its favor keeping in mind those that would and could not make it from out of town on our special day, based on the fact that the following day was a work day for most; therefore, presumably cutting the cost of the overall wedding. Oh well, so much for my budget. Saturday July 30th it is!

STORMING OUT

Are you serious? First me, then you, what is this? High School! I honestly did forget to pick up the money order. Remembering the many details of a wedding is enough to make anyone forget. Then add everything else into the equation. Kids, fiancé, home life, writing. It's a wonder I recall the minor specifics. So please forgive me if I forgot. Last time I checked I was still human, no robot parts here! I agree, sometimes I attempt to accomplish too many things throughout the course of the day, knowing that 24 hours is never enough! Doing my best to complete each thing does not make me a super being. I am learning so much about what it means to be engaged, a bride to be and soon a wife. I suppose of these lessons entails standing my ground no matter how angry, upset or disappointed I may be. Storming out is not an option, although this is what I did. It was not so much what he said, but more so the tone that caressed it. In a state of shock I stormed out of the house, not a minute before speaking my mind. My intentions were not to go far. Just put some distance in between the miscommunication and I. After walking once around the neighborhood I sought solace at the playground. I heard his steps approach but he never saw me. Probably in a panic he scanned the grounds over and not seeing me took off in the opposite direction. I was glad for the moment of solitude. Always trying to make everything right. When I got back he had not yet returned. When he did a tone like none other accompanied his presence. Worried? Yes. Concerned? Yes. Scared? Yes! He tried to talk to me, and when he had trouble breaching that wall, it was he that stormed out next. You gotta be kidding me!

HOW SWEET IT IS

After that temper tantrum we both threw, apologies were in order. The honey returned with gifts; the sweetest teddy bear and a box of Hershey's chocolates. I'm singing to myself "How sweet it is to be loved by him..." Hmmmmmmmm, sweeter than sweet. My life is richer than a box of chocolates!

CERTAINTY

If I don't know anything else, one thing I'm certain of is, if anything should happen to him I'd be lost. I would mournfully, but gladly throw myself into an infinitely forever dismal abyss! Misery would become my domicile. The occasional lack of communication, the sometimes erroneous use of words, the seldom upset... None of these things could ever alter the way I see him. He is perfect in each of his imperfections. It was certain at day 1 that I would love him for a lifetime.

PRIORITY

With fifty million templates and less than 6 months left, who has time to sift through unnecessary things (i.e. wedding checklists)? Herman and I have wandered purposely off of the beaten path and in doing so are listing as priority those components that comprise the key elements of our most perfect day. For him, the most important thing is the wow factor. This "WOW" is derived of the reception, the décor, the food, the drinks, and the party itself, period. As for me, I'm all about the statement. The veils, the tiara, the shoes, the flowers, and the final word of it all, photographs! With these elements up front, we create our own checklist.

NOT THAT IN LOVE

Of course as the tale goes, another trip to southeast Georgia was in order. Business and pleasure both were on the agenda this time. Of the utmost importance, we were on a wedding mission to scout out the ceremony & reception site. I suppose opinions differ when it comes to expectations! Let's just say mine were set way above the bar for this venue. I was getting multiple rave reviews, and had seen amazing photographs. It's no wonder my hopes for 'the perfect site' were set so high. Little did I know, the greater the expectation the bigger the disappointment. And disappointed I was. I had this picture perfect garden in my head for our outside summer wedding. I imagine viewing said site during the winter was not such a good idea. Everything was dead, cold, and grey... and I must admit, at this particular moment, I'm not that in love with the image that has replaced my once pretty painted picture.

THE IN LAW

Herman's in law to be, my oldest baby brother, has made the trip back with us. His family preceding him in the move, he himself has finally decided to relocate to the big city of Atlanta. The kids are excited to have their uncle around, Herman is glad for some male companionship and me, I'm just blessed to be his big sister!

WHAT GOES AROUND

... Comes around! Our 2nd V-day together has arrived. The best part about this Valentine's Day is the nature of company which I now keep. Being engaged to Herman has made this otherwise drab day extra sweet. I'm such a sucker for love but not particularly for surprises, so it's surprising that I would want to surprise him. Staying at home and opting out of the work force removes me from the traditional payroll, so my personal dollars are few at times. This in itself prompted me to save for the perfect gift on this special day, a bottle of 2008 Maestro Dobel Diamond Tequila! What better gift for the 'Mixologist' in my life?

SUSPICIOUS (BLING, BLING, BLING PT 2)

Acting extra weird raises questions and eyebrows alike. Claiming he had some files that needed to be copied, it didn't strike me as odd when he exited the house empty handed. That's half because I didn't notice until his return some time later. Coming back in empty handed probably raised more hairs on my neck than any scary movie ever could. The music changed as the score altered to match the thickness that suddenly filled the air. Herman must have known instinctively my first thought because he went into hyper-defense mode. He hates assumptions, especially those made toward him. Because of my suspicion his surprise has been ruined. To put my mind at ease he confirmed the nature of his outing. The ring, my apologies, the bling, bling, bling... he had went and purchased my ring. Now I feel like puppy poo, kinda. I still hate surprises and had I known, assumptions never would have been made. His explanation has turned into my anticipation as he refuses to tell me what my ring looks like. It has been sent to New York to be resized to fit my 9 ½ finger. I'm very excited and very sorry for jumping to conclusions, kinda!

UNCONDITIONAL

I just had a moment. It really is true that one rotten apple can spoil the whole bushel. But what if you've blindly eaten one bad fruit behind another? It tends to leave a bad taste in your mouth. One you'll sadly get used to. The nectar of this fruit is sweet on my tongue but unfamiliar to these lips. I love him, the heavens above know how much. But how do you let go of so much hurt from the past? How can I move on if I'm constantly waiting to be hurt? This is hard, but it's gotta be done. I've gambled in love, now I'm taking my chance again. It's time I, without a doubt, unequivocally trust him. Then and only then will this love be unconditional.

<u>HE IS</u>

Who's my best friend in the whole wide world? Of course it's him! He is my confidant, my buddy, my pal, my ace, my partner, my honey, my main squeeze, my lover, my best friend!

MARTINI, SHAKEN NOT STIRRED: A LATE VALENTINE

Another year, another valentine, another night out on the town! Our belated valentine dinner was highly anticipated. Chops was beckoning my palate. Of course, they did not disappoint. Valet was courteous, service was polite and prompt, and the environment had an exceptional ambience. Herman and I enjoyed drinks at the bar before being seated. The menu was filled with mouthwatering succulence. Our appetizer, jumbo lump crab which I had been craving since last valentine, and oyster rockerfeller. The latter dish was new to me, but I love seafood, so naturally I was game. His dinner, filet mignon and mashed potatoes. Mine, mushrooms and the seafood sampler complete with grilled salmon, scallops, jumbo lump crab, and South African lobster tail. Somebody pinch me, this is so sinfully delicious, it's almost unreal, my compliments to the chef! My favorite part of the night aside from being with the love of my life was the drinks. He ordered vodka infused raspberry lemonade and I ordered something grown and sexy. A martini, shaken not stirred. The wooden skewer that adorned the glass was embezzled with blue cheese filled olives. I'm so loving this night. Feeling like this is the life.

BACK AWAY FROM THE SCISSORS... AND THE DYE TOO

Those in my wedding party have been advised 2 decisions too late! A phone call to one of 'Las Tres Mejor Chicas' has revealed decision #1. My bestie has cut a few inches from her hair and judging the tone of her voice, she doesn't seem too thrilled about it. What began as a trim turned into a full blown haircut. Decision #2 is similar to the first but its delivery was much more dramatic. The soon to be sister in law has cut her hair as well. But cut is not the word that I would use to describe it, it's more of a chop! Newsflash, this just in, another of 'Las Tres Mejor Chicas' has accidentally dyed her hair black! Will the wedding party take note of this alert? Please! Be advised: Step away from the scissors and the dye too! You guys are clipping, cutting, chopping, & coloring your hair before 'my' big day. This affects your hairstyle on the day of, which in turn affects mine! Engagement photos have called attention to my own locks and the ever looming scissors have found their next victim... me!

COULD IT BE

Sleeping in late, the call was quite unexpected. Still hearing the amazing news, I welcomed the wakeup. Could it be? Is it possible we are going with plan Katandra? The details are sketchy to date but let's just say I know a woman who knows a woman who knows some people. What was my 'realistic' budget again? Let's make it happen!

DELIRIOUS SCRIBBLINGS & A VERY SPECIAL PLAYLIST

So I'm up at 4 a.m. writing in my diary. Why so late or early? It seems to be the only time I can get any peace and quiet. The house is still and I can actually hear myself think, feel myself breathe. It's the only time I can completely come undone. As I write I intentionally ignore the pile of dishes sitting in the sink, they can wait until daybreak. Instead I compile a very special playlist. The honey and I have decided on wedding favors, a cd of mixed music, his and my favorite love songs. I'm rather enjoying the search for good titles for 'Mr. & Mrs. 7.30.11 wedding playlist'. The mixture of tunes old and new and coffee encourages my hand to write despite my desire to sleep. So deliriously I listen, I drink and I continue to scribble.

EYE OF THE STORM

Where is the hole in this silver lined cloud? It's like I keep waiting for it to rain aggravation but joy continues to reign supreme. Don't get me wrong, I deserve every ounce of happiness that drizzles my way, but there is this sick feeling in the pit of my stomach. You know the feeling one gets during the eye of the storm? You know the calm is a mirage. The real threat? That ever prevalent beast, waiting to devour all in its path. It's kind of hard to smile when your senses are screaming "Something's not right!"

KALEIDOSCOPE

Have you ever tried looking through tear filled eyes? The view is askew at best. To say the least, the image that stands before you is greatly altered. No longer clear this visage, colors blend and objects meld. Just as I'm trying to let go of old hurts and tend to ancient wounds, learning to trust despite awaiting the arrival of the storm I know is quietly yet fast approaching. Now this! Kinda feeling like "I knew it was too good to be true". One thing being hurt teaches us is to never let your guard down and one thing life teaches us is to never let em see you cry! Well I have done both of these things. Curiosity has the power to kill more than an unsuspecting feline. It has the ability to kill the trust that has built up to keep nonsense out. There's that hole I had been looking for. It didn't peer from overhead as I thought it would. Instead it leaked through the wall he and I had worked so hard to build up to keep drama out. Text messages via his cell phone from some anonymous female I had never heard mention of has my nerves on end. Her name and number at my disposal she answered on the first ring. The purpose in the call, confirmation! Of what? I still don't know! Her response? Friends. Friends? I have no idea who this chic is! What may have come across as innocent to some was taken in offense by me. Rudely awakened, an answer from a sleepy fiancé was demanded. His explanation? The female is someone he met online long before he met me via the same site we met on, and since becoming engaged he has carried the 'friendship' over into our relationship, claiming it was of such unimportance he forgot to mention it. Frankly I don't like it. My body is physically aching and I can feel the vice of loves grip tight at my throat.

THIS FEELS LIKE A FRESH SCAR

The morning after is just as worst as the day before. It feels like I've been hit by a train! Although I allowed myself to be convinced that the friendship between him and any female is and never will be a cause for concern, I slept uneasily near him but not as close as I do on most nights. This hurt feels all too familiar. Old wounds exposed, this feels like a fresh scar! I don't mind him having friends but I don't want to feel like something is unmentioned on purpose, and I hate surprises. Bottling up my feelings on the matter has promised to be hazardous to him and me alike. Treading lightly on the conversation as not to relive the moment and go through that struggle once more. If nothing else, I'm glad he and I have the good sense not to let a problem go unsettled. Knowing that it would not resolve itself, we have talked through the 'misunderstanding'. The biggest accomplishment in this string of conversations has been me vocalizing how I feel about certain issues and his realizing he had gotten into a comfort groove and had unknowingly began taking all the little things for granted. Even in my pain I'm reminded to let him know that it's me who is his best friend and he better not be forgetting!

WHEN IT RAINS IT POURS

One upset after another is usually the way it goes. When it rains it pours. Well I'm letting it be known, one more straw on this already ladened back and i'm just gonna snap! Right about now I'm ready to change my name, apply for a visa, take a flight and pitch a tent somewhere... anywhere... but here. So many things to do, so much stress building up, all these surprises, no ceremony and reception site. I've misplaced the item number for 'Las Tres Mejor Chicas' dresses. Jade is being Jade. It must be flu season because the whole house has the sniffles. And I can still sense that storm brewing as if that shower was not enough. I don't know if this umbrella can handle any more bad weather. But like I said before, one upset after another is usually the way it goes. When it rains it pours.

THAT'S SOME SERIOUS HARDWARE
(BLING, BLING, BLING PT 3)

Feeling ill, Herman has taken a sick day from work. Perhaps the stress of all that is going on is beginning to get to him as well. I was unaware that my ring had made its trip back from New York. Finally she was to unite with her rightful owner. In spite of his shaky demeanor he was determined to place the ring on my finger when it returned. The jeweler made small talk as she boxed and bagged my naked finger adornment. I couldn't wait to get it on my hand. Outside, an eager Herman pauses beside the truck and in one swift movement removed the box from the bag and the ring from the box and was on one knee in the parking lot. Still a little salty I can feel my heart forgiving him for indiscretions. With ring in hand, he proposes, much more fairytale like than before! The ring, princess cut, 4 smaller square diamonds clustered together set inside prongs make up one big square diamond. The band and the big square are studded with round diamonds! This is some serious hardware! It's perfect, except, it's loose! Almost unable to bare parting with it, we appear before the jeweler once more. I hadn't noticed before, but she's the same jeweler who fitted my finger and sized me at a 9 ½. The ring is sent off because it's too small, returns too big, only to find out the 1st size was the correct size. Parting is such sweet sorrow so I've heard. Well I'm not giving it up! I'm not, I'm not, I'm not... at least not right now. A spacer has been temporarily placed on the ring so that I don't have to give it up so soon. I just wanna keep it, only for a little while. So pretty the way the light hits the diamonds and makes a million sparkles setting my hand on fire. Maybe I'll bring it back next week, maybe.

WINNING STREAK

I don't think I can take any more bad news. Herman's sister and I attended a bridal show a few weeks ago and had an absolute ball. Makeovers and cake tastings, I could have used this while that nasty storm was brewing! I signed up for several promotional giveaways but with so many brides in attendance, I doubted my chance of winning anything would be great. So you can imagine my delight at this unexpected gain. The first gift came in the form of a spa certificate for a facial. A phone call from yet another vendor presented more good fortune. We have won our choice of matching bands or a vacation for 2. Seems all of those kiosks I paused at and took the time to enter drawings and contests even if I didn't think my name was gonna be drawn really did pay off. Could it be that my luck is changing? I don't know but I sure hope so. I look to the horizon and tighten my grip on the umbrella handle, just in case clear skies are no more than a figment of my imagination.

MONOLOGUE

I've thought long and hard, and after having this one-sided conversation with myself I know exactly what it is I want to say to him. First of all there will be no more secrets and definitely no surprises. Opposite sex friends should be made aware of the depth of his and my relationship. "Hello! Engaged here!" We should have knowledge of each other's friends. Secondly, intimacy should not be a factor until all issues are resolved. Whoever said makeup sex is great sex was telling ½ truths. Physically yes, but sex between two people who love each other is not just physical. It's mental and emotional, all senses are engaged! So the last thing I want is to be on some weird roller coaster. There's enough going on under and between the sheets without adding that which goes on outside of them. I love Herman but I'm putting my foot down on this one. I refuse to be hurt by him because I feel that he is so much better than the pettiness of this situation and I believe that he and I are above foolishness! Last but not least, this 'friendship' he neglected to mention ends today, the same goes of any friendships I have with the opposite sex that he may feel uncomfortable with. Love = compromise. One thing I'm not relenting is this monologue I've memorized. When Herman gets in from work I'm giving him a piece of my mind and a pillow for the couch!

BEYOND AGGRAVATED

So this is the straw that has attempted to break the camel's back. Good thing I'm no camel! Still, I knew the weather was gonna get worse before it got better and here is the storm of the century! Its approach was slow and deliberate, but I could sense it near the whole time. The phone call, the dialogue, and each movement made thereafter were done so in slow motion. Calling to request an important document, my divorce decree from a previous marriage that went awry, turned out to be disastrous. What do you mean no record of the divorce? I filed the paperwork, I came to court, and I attended the parenting seminar! Did I forget to sign in blood? I can't take this! Seems the final court hearing was not attended by me, *he* never made it to any hearings. My only regret, an all-day internship on the final day of court and a calendar date that was obviously overlooked! I could literally feel my heart stop beating; it was as if I died a little in that moment. It was like watching a horror flick, only I was the victim. It was like seeing your favorite cashmere sweater unravel at the mere mention of any jagged little threat. Imagining those unsightly fibers promising to ruin my beloved sweater has me in panic mode. Now what? Back to square 1, block A, that's what. Wrap this up quick like and in a hurry. I have since resubmitted the case per the clerk. Lets finalize that chapter by any means necessary, and I do mean any! I'm not about to let a few loose strings deter my happiness. Sometimes when a thing has outgrown its season it's time it be replaced. I am looking forward to the end of winter.

THE END

I love to write but I have never been so glad to see the pages come to an end. With a new diary begins a new chapter and a new season in the life of this bride to be! I am looking forward to the end of winter and the 'Return of Spring'.

A CLOSING REMARK

In a world where so much technology is at our disposal, the written word is becoming more and more a thing of the past. I urge you to support your Local Libraries, Newspapers, Magazine Stands, Bookstores, Authors, Publishers and Literary Entities.

Keep the physical book from going extinct, and forever ignite the dream of *The Author & The Publisher...*

www.freedomink365.com

Connect with the CEO of FreedomInk

http://www.freedomink365.com/about_the_author

Tweet #READ365
http://twitter.com/#!/FreedomInk365

Follow us on Facebook
https://www.facebook.com/FreedomInkPublishing

The journey continues. See what happens next.
The Diary of A Bride To Be Book 2: The Return of Spring,
available NOW!

*All FreedomInk books available where awesome books
are sold.

www.ingramcontent.com/pod-product-compliance
Lightning Source LLC
LaVergne TN
LVHW011911080426
835508LV00007BA/481